A Survey of Syntax
in the
Hebrew Old Testament

by

J. WASH WATTS

Professor of Old Testament Interpretation
New Orleans Baptist Theological Seminary

WILLIAM B. EERDMANS PUBLISHING COMPANY
GRAND RAPIDS, MICHIGAN

PHOTOLITHOPRINTED BY GRAND RAPIDS BOOK MANUFACTURERS, INC.
GRAND RAPIDS, MICHIGAN
PRINTED IN THE UNITED STATES OF AMERICA

Preface to the Revised Edition

The original form of this work was published in 1951. In the thirteen years since that time no serious effort has been made to contradict its interpretation of the distinctive meanings in Hebrew verb forms and syntactical constructions. Some deficiencies have been pointed out by friendly critics; strong words of commendation have also been received. These developments have stimulated my desire to apply these interpretations in translation and in exegesis. One result has been the publication of *A Distinctive Translation of Genesis* in May, 1963, by Wm. B. Eerdmans Publishing Co. Similar works based upon this treatment of syntax are in progress.

Comparison of the treatment of Hebrew imperfects in the present work with the use of imperfects in Arabic has greatly strengthened my confidence concerning crucial features of the interpretation here given. I was able to make such comparison while teaching in Lebanon in 1961-62 and enjoying special opportunity for consideration of Arabic. This led to additions to the treatment of imperfects, the completion of the treatment of conditional sentences, extended treatment of dependent clauses, and many rearrangements intended to aid the study of all features by others.

Consideration of the following list of special features in this work should help a student to understand that the whole work is intended to give him keys to the interpretation of biblical Hebrew not found anywhere else:

(1) Distinctive translations for all perfects, which leave no need for the old theory that Hebrew used a *waw* consecutive with perfects at times.

(2) Distinctive translations for all imperfects, which leave no need for the old theory that *waw* consecutive makes the imperfect to which it is attached to receive the force of a preceding perfect or some other verb form. (This included a very important comparison with the use in Arabic of imperfects in past time and a consequent explanation of Exodus 3:14.)

(3) Distinctive translations for all participles, which leave no need for translation of any participle as though it were some other verb form.

(4) An interpretation of subjunctives so as to explain the combination of perfects with certain particles in conditional sentences and the combination of perfects with an interrogative pronoun in rhetorical questions

5

as furnishing expressions which are subjunctive in the sense of being contrary-to-fact.

(5) Distinctive translations for all types of cohortatives and jussives, which leave no occasion for failure to translate these forms according to their own nature.

(6) The addition of jussives of acquiescence to the various types of jussives previously described and consequent interpretations of Genesis 49:16-18; Isaiah 6:9-10, which should receive searching consideration in connection with our interpretation of predestination.

(7) Distinctive translations for all infinitives, which leave no need for interpreting an infinitive absolute as a substitute for an imperative, and which include this translation for Exodus 20:8: Remembering the sabbath day in order to keep it holy, *six days* you shall labor and do all your work.

(8) A treatment of all uses of *waw* conjunctive and *waw* consecutive so as to indicate a basic distinction between the two.

(9) A treatment of *waw* conjunctive with a perfect as having a correlative force in all cases.

(10) Explanation of *waw* consecutive as characteristic of narrative and of *waw* correlative as characteristic of prophecy.

(11) Detailed explanation and translation of relative clauses so as to illustrate the use of the relative particle and the pronouns used to introduce them.

(12) A new and consistent treatment of conditional sentences which makes it possible to remove subjective and inconsistent expressions in the translation of them. This treatment is applicable to all the legal ordinances stated in conditional form. Accordingly, a full translation of Exodus 21:2-14 is offered as proof of the claim made concerning this treatment.

The author owes a great debt of gratitude for aid and for use of his work on syntax by fellow workers in the department of Old Testament at the New Orleans Baptist Theological Seminary. These men are Dr. J. Hardee Kennedy, now Dean of the School of Theology, Dr. John Olen Strange, Dr. Thomas J. Delaughter, and Dr. George W. Harrison.

Dr. John D. W. Watts, who has taught Old Testament and Hebrew at the Baptist Theological Seminary, Ruschlikon-Zurich, Switzerland, since 1949, and who is now President, has likewise ontributed much helpful criticism and suggestion.

Dr. H. Leo Eddleman, who has been a teacher of Hebrew ugh many years, and who is now President of the New Or- Baptist Theological Seminary, has been most helpful and aging through more than thirty years.

—J. WASH WATTS

ans, Louisiana

Contents

Preface   5
Introductory Explanations   9
Abbreviations   10

Chapter One:
SENTENCE STRUCTURE IN SIMPLE SENTENCES   13
    I The Verb   13
    II Subjects   16
    III Accusatives   18
    IV Adverbial Phrases   22
    V Negatives   23
    VI Interrogatives   24
    VII Exclamations and Optative Expressions   24
    VIII Means of Expressing Special Emphasis   25

Chapter Two:
INTRODUCTORY MATTERS CONCERNING VERBS   28
    I State   29
    II Time   30
    III Mood   31
    IV Conclusion: Distinctive Translations   32

Chapter Three:
INDICATIVE PERFECTS   35
    I Simple Perfects   36
    II Previous Perfects   44
    III Characteristic Perfects   46
    IV Correlative Perfects   47

Chapter Four:
INDICATIVE IMPERFECTS   55
    I Frequentative Imperfects   56
    II Progressive Imperfects   58
    III Characteristic Imperfects   60
    IV Consecutive Imperfects   60

Chapter Five:
PARTICIPLES   70

Chapter Six:

SUBJUNCTIVES 74
   I Contrary-to-Fact Subjunctives 74
   II Potential Subjunctives 76
   III Optative Subjunctives 77

Chapter Seven:

IMPERATIVES 88
   I Imperative Imperfects 88
   II Imperatives Using the Special Form 89
   III Imperatives with *h* Added 90

Chapter Eight:

INFINITIVES 91
   I Infinitives Absolute 91
   II Infinitives Construct 94

Chapter Nine:

MEANS OF INTRODUCING INDEPENDENT CLAUSES 100
   I Use of the Conjunction *Waw* apart from Verbs 100
   II Co-ordinating Conjunctions in Comparative,
      Disjunctive, and Adversative Clauses 101
   III Uses of *Waw* with Verbs 103

Chapter Ten:

MEANS OF INTRODUCING DEPENDENT CLAUSES 118
   I In Subject and Object Clauses 118
   II In Relative Clauses 119
   III In Cause and Reason Clauses 126
   IV In Purpose and Result Clauses 129
   V In Circumstantial Clauses 130
   VI Types of Conditional Sentences 133
   VII Verbal Sequences in Conditional Sentences 134
   VIII A Comparison of Conditional Sentences in Exodus
      21:2-14 143
   IX Mixed Forms in Conditional Sentences 147

Selected Bibliography 151
Index of Biblical References 157

Introductory Explanations

Syntax (*syntaxis* in Latin; *suntaxis* in Greek; from *suntassein*, to put together in order) is "connected system or order."[1] With reference to language, it means the due arrangement of words in sentences and their agreement. This book is a survey of syntax in the Hebrew Old Testament. The arrangement of the book is as follows:

(1) In simple sentences, the basic facts concerning sentence structure are illustrated. Therefore a brief study of structure in simple sentences will be undertaken first.

(2) In compound sentences, the independent clauses are linked together by conjunctions. Old Testament usage gives a significance to these conjunctions that appears to be unique in the field of language. This significance depends in large measure upon the nature of the verbs with which they are used. It is necessary, therefore, to undertake an extensive, thorough, and sharply defined appraisal of the distinctive meanings in these verbs before the compound sentences as a whole are treated. When they are finally examined completely, the distinctive meanings of the conjunctions can also be defined.

(3) In complex sentences, the dependent clauses come into view. In the dependent clauses, the relations between conjunctions and prepositions on the one hand and the moods of verbs on the other involve many complex arrangements of words and clauses that are dependent for their meaning upon comparison with their use in independent clauses. The study of these complex arrangements must come last.

1 *Webster's New International Dictionary of the English Language,* (2nd ed.; Springfield: G. & C. Merriam Company, 1944), p. 2560.

Abbreviations

(Periods are omitted for the sake of brevity)

GENERAL

ASV — American Standard Version
AT — An American Translation
AV — Authorized Version
BDB — Brown, Driver, and Briggs
DV — Douay Version
ERV — English Revised Version
Eng — English
Heb — Hebrew
MNT — Moffatt's New Translation
RSV — Revised Standard Version

TECHNICAL

Note: The chief purpose of these abbreviations is to make possible the syntactical summaries given at the close of discussion concerning each construction mentioned. Another purpose is to facilitate the use of footnotes. These abbreviations may also be used in class work by teachers or pupils to summarize rapidly their own conclusions concerning the syntax of any construction. Standing alone, many of them appear ambiguous; but in the combinations in which they appear, the proper meaning is obvious because of the context.

abs — absolute
acc — accusative
acq — acquiescence
act — active
adj — adjective
adv — adverb
app — apposition
art — article
ass — asseverative
cau — cause, causal
cer — certainty
ch — characteristic
cir — circumstance, circumstantial
cl — clause
coh — cohortative

com — complete, completeness, command, common
comp — compulsory, complement, comparison
con — confidence, contrary-to-fact, consent, construct
cond — condition, conditional
conj — conjunction, conjunctive
cons — consecutive
cont — continuous, continuance, contrast
co-or — co-ordinate
cor — correlative
dat — dative
dec — decree
dem — demonstrative
dep — dependent
des — desire
det — determination
dir — direct
dis — discourse
em — emphatic
ell — elliptical
exc — exclamation
exh — exhortation
fre — frequentative
fut — future
gen — genitive
imp — imperfect
imv — imperative
inc — incomplete, incipient
ind — indicative, indirect, indefinite, independent
inf — infinitive
int — interrogative, intensity, introducing
jus — jussive
lim — limitation
lit — literally
log — logical
man — manner

n — noun
nar — narrative
nat — nature
nec — necessity
neg — negative
obj — object
opt — optative
pa — past
pas — passive
per — permission, personal
pet — petition
pf — perfect
phr — phrase
pl — place
plu — plural
pos — possibility
pot — potential
pre — present
prev — previous
pred — predicate
prep — preposition
priv — privative
pro — prophetic, pronoun, probable
prog — progressive
pt — participle
pur — purpose
rea — reason
rel — relative
req — request
res — result, responsibility
rhe — rhetorical
sen — sentence
seq — sequence
sing — singular
sp — specific, special
sub — subject, subsequent, subordinate
subj — subjunctive
suf — suffix

sug — suggestion
sum — summary
syn — syntax, syntactical
tem — temporal
tran — translation, translated
und — understood
vb — verb
wil — willingness

Chapter One

Sentence Structure in Simple Sentences

In the study of simple sentences we need to summarize many scattered facts arising out of previous studies of grammar. Here and there some of the more intricate details need to be added.

Following normal word order, verbs are treated first, then subjects with modifiers, then objects with modifiers. In case there are two objects, it is understood that the more important comes first.

I

THE VERB

In a simple sentence only one verb is in question, for each Hebrew verb makes a clause of its own. In translation we may compress several separate clauses into one; but in the original, except in rare uses of participles, they are separate by reason of the fact that each Hebrew verb carries its subject with it. Thus we deal here with the relation of a single verb to its subject or subjects.

1. The connection between subject and predicate is expressed in the following:
   (1) A regular verb:
      Gen. 1:1— . . . God *created* . . . .
      Gen. 1:2a — and the earth *was* waste and void.
   (2) The verb "to be" understood:
      Gen. 1:2b — And darkness (*was*) upon the face of the deep.
      Gen. 28:13, 15 — . . . I (am) Yahweh . . . . And behold, I (am) with you.

13

The verb is written in parentheses in these translations to show that it was not in the Hebrew. No verb of any kind appeared in the original written statement. Yet there was undoubtedly an unexpressed idea signified by the placing of two substantives, two nouns or a pronoun and a noun, together in this way. Contexts make it clear that such a statement was understood as a declaration or a denial that the two substantives are identified. The Hebrew seemingly felt no need for further expression in making such a statement. Thus we have what some grammarians have called a substantive or nominative sentence. It may be easier for some to think of these expressions as implying the verb "to be" in some form. In such cases we can say that the verb "to be" is understood, i.e., contained in the author's thought but not expressed in a word.

A somewhat similar expression appears at times when users of English are making introductions. The statement "Mr. Jones, — Mr. Smith!" means, of course, Mr. Jones, this is Mr. Smith. Even as the demonstrative pronoun "this" is omitted in the first sentence, so one of the substantive forms is often omitted in the Hebrew sentences. Thus, "I (am) with you" in Gen. 28:15 means "I am the one with you," or else "I am one who is for you, at hand and on your side."

These expressions are used frequently in Hebrew, and they should be considered quite normal. Perhaps the uses of "to be" in past or present time that have an emphatic word before them are the ones to be considered unusual. The description of the earth in Gen. 1:2a as a thing that was "waste and void" is an example, for "earth" was placed emphatically, i.e., before the verb. Unless the verb was written, one could not tell that the author was expressing emphasis. The author used this verb "to be" in an unusual way in order to emphasize its subject.

In future time, the Hebrew authors wrote out the verb "to be." The purpose appeared to be that of using it as a specific expression of frequentative or progressive action. Therefore, Jacob, when reflecting upon the promises Yahweh made to him at Bethel, said, "Seeing that Yahweh *will continue to be* with me . . ." (Gen. 28:20). Therefore, two of the great promises contained in the initial statement of Yahweh's covenant with Israel were written thus: " . . . and as for you, *you will become* for me a kingdom of priests and a holy nation"

(Ex. 19:6). Such use of "to be" in future time likewise reflects the fact that omission of "to be" is the normal usage in past and present time.

(3) A personal pronoun in the third person, no matter what the person of the subject:

Deut. 12:23 — For the blood (3rd per) *it* is the life; or, For the blood is the life.

II Sam. 7:28 — Thou (2nd per) art *he,* The (One True) God; or, Thou art The (One True) God.

Zech. 4:5 — Do you know what *they,* even these, are? or, Do you know what these are?

(4) The following particles:

yesh, there is

Job 11:18 — *There is* hope.

'en, there is not

Ex. 5:16 — Straw *is not* given.

hinneh, behold

Gen. 18:19 — *Behold,* in the tent!

2. Agreement of subject and verb appears as follows:

(1) A verb that precedes its subject may agree with it in gender and number, or appear in the third masculine singular without regard for the gender and number of the subject:

Isa. 47:1 — Yea, *there shall come* (3rd mas sing) *evil* (fem sing).

Mic. 2:6 — *Reproaches* (fem plu and written last in Heb) *will not depart* (3rd mas sing).

Ps. 119:137 — *Right are* (3rd mas sing) *thy judgments* (mas plu).

(2) A verb that follows its subject agrees with it in gender and number, as a rule:

Gen. 1:2a — *The earth* (fem sing) *was* (fem sing) waste . . . .

(3) A verb with a dual subject is usually in the plural but occasionally in the feminine singular, because there is no dual form of the verb:

Isa. 1:15 — *Your hands are full* (com plu) of blood.

I Sam. 4:15 — And *his eyes were dim* (fem sing).

(4) When any word, even a pronominal suffix, comes between the verb and the subject, the question of agreement is frequently disregarded. Examples are found in I Sam. 4:15;

Joel 1:20; Isa. 34:13; Ps. 103:5. (This practice has been pointed out in recent years by G. R. Driver.)

(5) A verb with a compound subject including a genitive used in connection with *kol,* all, agrees with that genitive; it may do so with a genitive used in connection with *qol,* voice; and it may do so in poetry whenever the author desires to emphasize the genitive:

> Gen. 5:5 — And all (nom) of the days (gen) of Adam came to be (plu) nine hundred and thirty years.
>
> Gen. 37:35 — And all his sons and all his daughters rose up (plu) to comfort him.
>
> Gen. 4:10 — The voice of thy brother's blood (lit, bloods) is crying out (plu).
>
> I Sam. 2:4 — A bow of mighty men is broken (plu).

(6) A verb with two or more subjects joined by *waw* may agree with one and be understood with the other, or it may be in the plural to express agreement with them taken together:

> Num. 12:1 — Then proceeded to speak (sing) Miriam and Aaron.
>
> I Sam. 31:7 — Saul and his sons died (plu).

(7) A verb with a collective noun may be singular or plural, although the plural is more frequent. An author may switch back and forth in the same passage:

> Ex. 33:8-11 — *All the people proceeded to stand* (plu), and *they took their stations* (plu), each at the door of his tent; . . . and *all the people saw* (sing) the pillar of cloud; . . . and *all the people rose up* (sing), and they worshipped (plu), each at the door of his tent.

(8) A verb with a plural subject denoting a group, each member of which is characterized by a certain action, may be in the singular to make the predicate apply to each member. Cf. Num. 24:9; Ex. 31:14. Hebrew authors shift in various ways from general to individual subjects or from individual to general ones. Sometimes this occurs several times in one sentence, apparently for variety.

II

Subjects

1. An ordinary subject is represented by the following:
    (1) A noun:

Gen. 2:6 — And *a mist* proceeded to go up.

(2) A pronoun or pronominal suffix joined to a particle:

II Sam. 7:28 — *Thou* art God.

Gen. 6:13 — And *behold I* am bringing destruction on them.

(3) An adjective used as a noun:

Ps. 4:7; 4:6 in Eng — *Many are saying,* Who can show us any good?

(4) An adverb that assumes the force of a noun:

II Sam. 1:4 — *Many* of the people have fallen.

"Many" represents the Hebrew word *harbeh,* which is regularly used as an adverb meaning greatly or exceedingly. Here, however, as in Jer. 42:2 and a few other instances, it is construed as a noun. The possibility of such a change arises out of the fact that this adverb originated as an infinite absolute, which may serve both as an adverb and a noun.

(5) A prepositional phrase modifying an indefinite subject:

Ex. 16:27 — *Some* of the people went out.

A literal translation in this case would be, "They from the people went out." "From the people" is not an adverbial phrase modifying "went out"; rather, it is a restrictive phrase modifying "they." The persons indicated by "they" are not identified in any other way by the context. "From the people" is therefore so identified with "they" as to be an essential part of the subject.

2. An indefinite subject may be represented by the following:

(1) A verb in the third person, masculine, singular or plural:

Ps. 126:2 — Then *they said* among the nations . . . .

Isa. 9:5, 9:6 in Eng — And *one* (or *men*) will call his name . . . .

(2) A verb with a participle from its root for a subject:

Deut. 22:8 — If *any man should fall* from thence (lit, if *one* falling *should fall* from thence), . . .

(3) The pronoun of the second person singular:

Gen. 13:10 — Like the land of Egypt when *you come* to Zoar.

3. An impersonal subject is represented by a verb in the third person. When reference to nature is made, the verb is always feminine. Otherwise, the verb is usually masculine; and if passive,

always masculine. Our neuter pronoun "it" is used for translation in these cases:

Amos 4:7 — On one piece *it rained* (fem).

Job 3:13 — If I had slept [the sleep of death], then *it had been rest to me.*

Isa. 53:5 — By reason of his stripes *there shall be healing* for us (lit, *it shall be healed* for us).

III

ACCUSATIVES

Any noun in the predicate governed by the verb rather than a preposition must be construed by us as an accusative. In translation, however, it is necessary to put with many of these nouns such prepositions as English uses with genitives, datives, or accusatives. The history of many Hebrew words shows that Hebrew usage has varied in its use of prepositions with these words, sometimes using one, sometimes not doing so. Accordingly, our addition of prepositions for the sake of English minds is not contrary to Hebrew thought, but it renders explicit what is implicit in the Hebrew.

II Kings 8:13 furnishes an instructive example. Translated literally it reads this way: Yahweh has caused me to see you king. "Me" is the object of the causative action of the verb; "you" is object of "see," the root idea of the verb; and "king" is an adverbial accusative, describing the condition in which "you" is seen. When we translate thus: "Yahweh has shown you to me as king"; we leave "you" as a direct object, not needing a preposition; we turn "me" into an indirect object and therefore put "to" with it; and we put "as" with "king," making it into an adverbial phrase.

These accusatives may be classified mainly by their service as direct objects of the verb or as adverbial accusatives that specify some particular aspect of the verbal state. Among double accusatives and cognate accusatives both types are found.

1. Object accusatives:

Gen. 1:1 — God created *the heavens and the earth.*

Gen. 6:2 — And they proceeded to take *for themselves wives.*

II Kings 8:13 — Yahweh has shown *to me you* as king, or Yahweh has given *to me a vision of you* as king.

A variation in the use of prepositions with the object accusatives needs to be observed carefully. A direct object, like "heavens" in Gen. 1:1, does not need a preposition. An indirect object, however, may or may not receive one in Hebrew. In Gen. 6:2 "for" is written in Hebrew with "themselves," but in II Kings 8:13 no preposition is written with "me."

Omission of prepositions is regular in Hebrew composition when any other type of adverbial accusative is used. Accusatives of specification of all kinds and also cognate accusatives are thus written. Accusatives of specification, however, do require prepositions in English. The translator, therefore, must take care to discern the preposition that fits the context.

2. Accusatives of specification:

These accusatives are called accusatives of specification because each one specifies the particular reference of the verbal action or state in its sentence. That reference may be to place, time, limitation, condition, manner, means, or result. The context must be relied upon for indicating what kind of reference is specified, and the translator must supply the preposition that helps to make it clear.

(1) Specifying place:

Gen. 45:25 — And they proceeded to come *into the land* of Canaan.

Gen. 33:18 — And he proceeded to camp *before the city*.

Gen. 18:1 — And he was sitting *at the entrance* to the tent.

I Kings 18:32 — And he proceeded to build the stones (dir obj) *into an altar* (adv acc of pl whither).

Ps. 3:8 — Thou shalt smite all my enemies (dir obj) *on the cheek-bone* (adv acc of pl where).

Prepositions answering to the question, Whither? include to, into, out of, and the like. Prepositions answering to the question, Where? include before, at, in, on, by, beside, and the like.

(2) Specifying time:

Ps. 1:2 — He meditates *day and night*.

Gen. 5:3 — And Adam continued to live *for a hundred and thirty years*.

Concise wording may omit prepositions, as in Ps. 1:2, but it is possible to add them, saying, "by day and by night."

(3) Specifying limitation of distance, number, place, and so forth:

> Gen. 7:20 — *Fifteen cubits above* them . . . the waters prevailed.
>
> Amos 5:3 — The city going forth *up to a thousand* will leave a remnant *up to a hundred,* and the one going forth *up to a hundred* will leave a remnant *up to ten.*

(4) Specifying condition:

> Amos 2:16 — *As one stripped naked* will he flee in that day.
>
> I Sam. 15:32 — And Agag proceeded to go to him *with confidence.*
>
> Gen. 37:35 — I shall go down to my son *in mourning.*

(5) Specifying manner:

> Ps. 56:3 — Many are fighting against me *in pride.*
>
> Gen. 46:2 — And they proceeded to bow down to him *with their faces to the ground.*
>
> Gen. 32:31 — I have seen God *face to face.*
>
> Prov. 22:23 — And he shall spoil those spoiling them (dir obj) *as to the soul* (adv acc of man).

(6) Specifying means:

> Isa. 1:20 — *By the sword* you will be devoured.
>
> Ps. 139:14 — *For by wonders* am I distinguished.
>
> Gen. 2:7 — And Yahweh proceeded to form the man (dir obj) *out of dust* (adv acc of means).
>
> Ex. 6:3 — *By means of my name Yahweh* I did not make myself known to them.

(7) Specifying result:

> Zech. 14:4 — And the mount of Olives shall be split *so as to be a great valley.*
>
> I Sam. 5:9 — And the hand of Yahweh began to be upon the city *so as to be a very great confusion.*
>
> Hag. 2:11 — Ask the priests (dir obj) *for instruction* [*so as to get instruction*] (adv acc of res).

3. Cognate accusatives:

> Ex. 29:9 — And you shall gird them (dir obj) *with girdles* (cog acc, also acc of means).

A noun from the same root as its verb is frequently put with that verb as a cognate accusative. This appears to be done in order to give a concrete example of the verbal action or added information about it.   Thus these cognate accusatives are essentially adverbial accusatives.

The translation of these cognate accusatives requires care because users of English dislike such repetition.   Usually a word that is cognate in significance but not in stem can be found to represent the accusative.   In Gen. 1:29 we may translate thus: "an herb producing seed," rather than saying: "an herb seeding seed." At times, as in Zech. 8:2 and II Sam. 19:5, Hebrew itself uses accusatives which are cognate in significance only.   We may easily make this practice general.   Oftentimes a suitable preposition must be added.   Cf. Gen. 37:5; II Sam. 7:7; 13:36; Jer. 22:19.

4. Use of *'eth* with accusatives:

When it is desired to point to a word as specially important, *'eth* is used before the thing defined.   Thus it is used in the following ways:

(1) Generally before a direct object if it is definite (Cf. Gen. 1:4.   Particularly is this true when the direct object is placed before the verb.)

(2) Before words which by nature specify definite things
a. The following pronouns:
'asher, who, which, or what (Gen. 9:24).
Strictly speaking, this word is the particle of relation, but it serves as a pronoun.
zeh, this (Lev. 11:4)
mi, who (Isa. 6:8)
The fact that *'eth* never appears before *mah,* what, emphasizes the fact that it is used to mark that which is definite. Whereas *mi* is used to identify persons and is always definite, *mah* is used to refer to the nature of things and is indefinite.

b. Certain words which at times are used to specify individuals:
kol, when meaning each (Deut. 2:34)
'asher, other (Jer. 16:13)
'echadh, one (I Sam. 9:3)

c. A noun or a singular pronoun unaccompanied by an article and used to typify a group (Ex. 21:28; Isa. 41:7; 50:4).

d. Designations of particular time (Ex. 13:7) or place (Judg. 19:18).

e. Adverbial accusatives that locate a verbal state (I Kings 15:23; 17:25).

(3) Before words that identify the subject or object more clearly or fully (Gen. 27:42; Judg. 20:44; I Sam. 26:16; II Sam. 11:15; Ezek. 17:21).

IV

Adverbial Phrases

1. Adverbial phrases introduced by a preposition:

In addition to any phrase composed of an ordinary noun with a preposition and used to modify a noun, adjective, or adverb, there must be included here those phrases composed of infinitives construct with prepositions. These occur very frequently in Hebrew, and in English they are usually turned into various kinds of clauses. So far as construction is concerned, they are adverbial phrases.

2. Adverbial phrases expressing comparative or superlative degree:

The comparative degree is expressed by use of the preposition *min,* from, prefixed to the second word involved in the comparison, as in Gen. 29:30. The superlative degree is expressed in the following ways:

(1) By use of the phrase *mikkol,* from all, as in Gen. 3:1 and Job 1:3.

(2) By use of the preposition *be,* among, with the second of the nouns compared, as in Song of Sol. 1:8.

(3) By emphatic use of the positive accompanied by the article, as in the clause "David was the smallest" (I Sam. 17: 14); or by emphatic use of the positive with another noun in construct relation, as in the expression "the three oldest" (I Sam. 17:14); or by emphatic use of the positive with a pronominal suffix attached (Jonah 3:5).

(4) By ordinary use of nouns in construct relation, when the first is the singular and the latter the plural of the same noun, as in Gen. 9:25; or when there is a partitive relation between the nouns, as in Jonah 3:5.

3. Adverbial phrases using *h* directive to indicate the place whither an action leads (Gen. 14:10) or the place where it happens (I Kings 4:14).

V

NEGATIVES

Negative particles appear immediately before the words they negate. Even the verb is preceded by its negative, for negatives are emphatic by nature.

1. *lo'*, not, is strongly declarative and with the imperative imperfect is prohibitory. It is widely used with verbs. Occasionally it appears before a noun or an adjective (Deut. 32:6, 21), giving a meaning like the prefixes un-, in-, and im-. Perhaps the Hebrews thought of it in these situations as followed by the verb to be. In Num. 16:29 we may use the verb to be after *lo'* and the relative pronoun after *YHWH*.

2. *'al*, do not, is contingent in nature and is used with cohortatives and jussives.

3. *terem*, not yet, is used with verbs only (Gen. 2:5).

4. *lebhilti*, in order that . . . not, is the regular negative with infinitives (Gen. 4:15; Deut. 17:19, 20). Rarely is it used with other forms, and the relative pronoun is to be understood as being with it in such cases (Ex. 20:20). When used with nouns it is sometimes equivalent to "without" (Isa. 14:6).

5. *'en*, there is not, is the construct form of *'ayin*, nothing. It is used regularly with nouns and participles and occasionaly with infinitives. When a participle needs a negative, *'en* is nearly always used. When it appears with an infinitive, the infinitive is a noun (Ps. 40:6). With a noun it is equivalent to "without" (Joel 1:6).

6. *beli*, 'not,' and its short form *bal* are used like *lo'*. *bal* occurs only in poetry. *beli* with nouns is equivalent to without (Job 8:12).

7. *belo'*, without, is practically always with nouns (Isa. 55:1). Once, in Num. 35:23, it occurs with an infinitive, the particle serving as a preposition and the infinitive as a noun.

8. Combinations of these particles (I Kings 10:21; II Kings 1:3; Isa. 5:9).

9. A negative combined with *kol,* all, or *'ish,* each one, to express the idea of nothing or no one (Ps. 49:18; I Sam. 11:13).

VI

INTERROGATIVES

Interrogatives, like negatives, come first in Hebrew sentences.

1. Interrogative Particles:
    (1) *ha,* which does not imply an answer (Gen. 4:9; 8:8; 24:58).
    (2) *halo',* which does imply an affirmative answer (Ex. 14:12).

2. Interrogative Pronouns:
    (1) *mi,* who?, always refers to the identification of persons (II Sam. 23:15; Ps. 24:10). Any noun with this interrogative, which is not directly personal, will be found to refer to a name or other identification of a person (Gen. 33:8; Judg. 13:7).
    (2) *mah,* what?, always refers to the nature of a person or thing (Zech. 1:9). It is used in the sense of wherefore to express reproach (Ex. 17:2); in the sense of how to express objection or doubt (Job 9:2); with *le* and the first person to deny connection with something (I Kings 12:16); with *le* and the second person to express condemnation (Isa. 3:15).
    (3) *'ezeh,* which?, also refers to things (I Kings 13:12).

3. Interrogative Adverbs:
    (1) *mathay,* when? (Gen. 30:30).
    (2) *'ekhah,* how?, inquires as to manner (Deut. 18:21).
    (3) *kammah,* how much?, how long? (Gen. 47:8).
    (4) *lammah,* wherefore?, why?, inquires as to purpose (Ex. 2:13).
    (5) *maddua',* why?, inquires as to cause (Isa. 5:4).
    (6) Combinations of various kinds (Gen. 16:8; Jer. 5:7).

VII

EXCLAMATIONS AND OPTATIVE EXPRESSIONS

Exclamations are of course emphatic. There is no verb for them to precede, but they do precede whatever else there may be in the phrase (I Sam. 23:20; Gen. 43:20; Isa. 5:20; Joel 1:15; Gen. 43:23; Num. 14:28; Gen. 18:25).

Among the optative expressions are the following: the particle *lu* (Gen. 17:18; 23:13; Num. 14:2); the particle *'im* (Ps. 139: 19); and the pronoun *mi* with an imperfect, especially in the expression *mi yitten,* who would give? (II Sam. 23:15; Ex. 16:3).

VIII

MEANS OF EXPRESSING SPECIAL EMPHASIS

In addition to expressions that are by nature emphatic, i.e., negative, interrogative, and exclamatory expressions, the following ways of expressing special emphasis are used:

1. Unusual word order:

   Gen. 1:2a — And *the earth* was waste and void.

   In this case Hebrew indicates the emphasis by placing the subject before the verb. English composition can do the same thing by means of underscores in a manuscript and italics in print.

   Gen. 3:10 — *Your voice* I heard in the garden.

   Here the direct object is before the verb.

   Gen. 4:6 — Therefore Yahweh proceeded to say *to Cain,* "For what reason are you angry?"

   The indirect object is before the direct object, which is the entire statement in quotation marks. All indirect objects placed before direct objects are emphatic in some degree. In this case we see a method used quite frequently with quotations by which attention is called to the person addressed in the quotation.

   Gen. 4:7 — *At the very door* sin is lying in wait.

   Here an adverbial phrase is placed in a position of strong emphasis.

   Gen. 3:14 — *Because you have done this, cursed* are you.

   The reason clause is placed ahead of the main clause. It places strong emphasis, therefore, upon the fact that God's judgment was based upon the deeds of the Serpent, not merely upon his possibilities or tendencies.

   "Cursed" appears in a substantive expression, one with the verb "to be" understood. Since there is no written verb to mark the position of other words as regular or irregular, the question of emphasis faces circumstances for which previous observations have not prepared us. They need to be studiously observed wherever they appear.

The ordinary statement in this case would be: "You are cursed." The whole statement is addressed to the Serpent, so the ordinary statement would start with the personal pronoun referring to him. Whenever the normal order of the two substantives in such a statement is reversed, the purpose appears to be emphasis upon the one placed first.

Gen. 9:26 — *Blessed* is Yahweh, the God of Shem.

"Blessed" is a participle. Since participles are inflected like nouns, they often serve as predicate complements. In such cases they are one of the two substantives in a substantive sentence, and the verb "to be" understood links the two as in any other substantive sentence. Moreover, reversal of normal word order indicates emphasis. Normal order in this instance would put Yahweh before the verbal form. The reverse order puts the emphasis on "blessed."

2. Repetition:

(1) Repetition of a noun, like Yahweh in Ex. 34:6 or earth in Jer. 22:29.

(2) Repetition of verb forms, using an infinitive absolute with the finite verb, usually an infinitive absolute of the same root and stem.

If the infinitive absolute precedes the verb, as in Ex. 19:5, it emphasizes the certainty of the verbal action or state. The conditional clause, therefore, means this: "If you will *indeed* harken, . . ." If the infinitive absolute follows the verb, as in Isa. 6:9, it emphasizes continuance or the like. The word of the prophet, therefore, was to be this: "Hear you, *keeping on hearing,* but do not understand."

(3) Repetition of the reference to a distant antecedent by placing a noun in apposition with a personal pronoun that refers to it:

Ex. 2:6 — Then she proceeded to open (it) and to see *him, even the child.* (The antecedent is "son" in v. 5)

(4) Repetition of the reference to an emphatic antecedent by means of the demonstrative pronoun "these, i.e., the same."

Gen. 6:4 — *The Nephilim* were in the earth in those days . . . , *the same* were the mighty men that were of old.

(5) Repetition of a pronoun, either as a separate pronoun, or a pronominal suffix, as in Job 1:15; II Sam. 17:5; Ps. 27:2:

Job 1:15 — And *I* only escaped, *even I alone,* to tell you.

(6) Placing a word or phrase independently at the beginning of the sentence, without grammatical connection with what follows, and resuming reference to it later by one of the following means:

   a. *Waw* used as a demonstrative adverb:

     Isa. 6:1 — *In the year that king Uzziah died, then* I began to see the Lord.

   b. Both *waw* and a pronoun:

     Gen. 22:24 — *And his concubine,* whose name was Reumah, *even she also,* proceeded to bear Tebah.

3. The pronoun *hu'*, referring to a subject already stated, as in Lev. 17:11 and Isa. 7:14:

Isa. 7:14 — Therefore the Lord *himself* will give you a sign.

This use of *hu'* is to be distinguished from that of *hahu'*, which means that, or, the same.

4. Use of a pronoun with the preposition *le* after verbs. This usage indicates that the action of the verb refers in particular to one specified by the pronoun as in Gen. 12:1 and Isa. 31:8:

Gen. 12:1 — Get *yourself* out from your land, from your kinsfolk, and from your father's household. . . .

5. Identification with a specially important thing or person, marked by addition of the definite article:

I Kings 18:17 — Is it *you, the one troubling* Israel?

Isa. 37:16 — Thou art *God* (lit, Thou art *he, The* [One True] *God.*)

The substantive sentence is used for identification. There is, however, no inverted word order. The great significance of the words put in apposition with the pronoun arises out of the context, and the article or other expression of definiteness calls special attention to it.

Chapter Two

Introductory Matters Concerning Verbs

The position of the verb in the Hebrew sentence is an indication of its importance in syntax as well as in the more fundamental parts of grammar. In the study of etymology and accidence the verb is given a major portion of our attention, not merely because its construction is difficult for those unfamiliar with Semitic thought-forms, but because the understanding of its significance is essential to an understanding of its sentence. Therefore, we also put it first in syntax, and afterwards we turn to sentence structure as a whole.

The syntax of Hebrew verbs is dominated by the following factors: (1) state, (2) time, (3) mood, (4) voice.

Voice is so clearly associated in introductory grammar with the stems of the verb that there is doubtless no need for further treatment. The other three characteristics, however, must be more carefully examined.

The sources of evidence in this examination may be broadly distinguished as follows: (1) evidence of the state appears usually in the grammatical construction of the verb alone, but at times additional evidence is in the context; (2) evidence of the time appears in the context only; (3) evidence of the mood appears as a rule in the verb and the context.

Definitions of state, time, and mood must be sharply drawn in the light of this evidence if translation is to be accurate. Furthermore, it appears advisable to define each point in terms that will enable the reader to judge it separately from each other point because one's choice of translation will often depend upon a separate judgment concerning each point. First of all, therefore, general definitions will be undertaken; then the varied developments can be examined.

28

I

STATE

State, as used at present and generally in this work, means condition of action, mind, body, or event. Let this use of the word "state" be carefully observed. Occasionally it will be necessary to distinguish certain actions and states, setting them in contrast with each other, as in the comparison of stative and active verbs. Here the word "state" is much broader. It applies to the condition indicated by any verb, active or stative, and describes that condition in a general sense as complete, incomplete, or continuous.

In formulating our judgments concerning state, we observe first of all these simple facts: a perfect indicates a complete state, i.e., one that is finished or established; an imperfect indicates an incomplete state, i.e., one that is not finished and so in beginning, or is not established and so subject to interruptions and repetitions; a participle indicates a continuous state, i.e., one in progress but not subject to interruptions. Inasmuch as imperatives have the same ground form as imperfects, they also indicate incomplete states.

After this preliminary observation about state, we proceed to examine time and mood in turn. Certain evidence as to time helps us to decide concerning mood. For instance, if a perfect is in future time and also in an interrogative sentence, this combination indicates a subjunctive mood. Likewise, certain evidence concerning time and mood helps us to make a more precise appraisal of the state. For instance, if a perfect is in past time and there is with it a particle indicating a subjunctive mood, we know that the state, though viewed as complete, is contrary to fact. In connection with all subjunctives and imperatives, the state contemplated by the author is merely a mental state, not yet realized in any sense; therefore, state and mood are inevitably linked together as two sides of the same thing. In view of this identification of state and mood, we can observe that perfects indicate contrary-to-fact states, imperfects indicate potential states or states that are optative in the sense of being desired, and imperatives indicate states that are imperative in the sense of being compulsory.

Infinitives are not mentioned because they are never really verbs. They develop as verb forms and partake of certain verbal characteristics, but their true nature is nominal or adverbial. They will be treated later as adverbs and gerunds.

The state of the verb is generally, but not always, indicated by its grammatical form.   A perfect standing alone, as it nearly always does, indicates a completed state; but with certain particles it indicates the opposite extreme, a contrary-to-fact state.   Under ordinary circumstances an imperfect indicates an incomplete state; however, circumstances appearing in the context may indicate that the state is not actually begun but merely potential; likewise, other circumstances may indicate that its state is optative.   A participle indicates a continuous state.   An imperative indicates a compulsory state.

II

TIME

The time of the Hebrew verb must be judged in the light of its context.   There are no obvious markers in grammatical formation or syntactical arrangement.   The reader must view the context as a whole, whether it be a sentence, a paragraph, a passage, a book, or a sphere of knowledge, and discern the time that fits.

Time, as used here, is that which distinguishes the state of the verb as before, now, or after.

A time which is related to a single time viewpoint, i.e., before, now, or after the time of the author, and not also before or after some other time, will be designated by a single or simple name, as a past, a present, or a future:

Gen. 1:1 — In the beginning God *created* (a pa) the heavens and the earth.

Gen. 4:10 — The voice of your brother's blood *is crying* (a pre) unto me.

Gen. 4:14 — And from thy face *I shall be hid* (a fut).

A time which is related both to the time of the author and to another time will be designated by a compound name, as previous present or subsequent past.   Let it be observed that both parts of these names indicate time.   Names like present perfect and future perfect are not used in the designation of time because they mix the idea of state with that of time.   It is desired that each point of syntax be judged separately.

A previous past is a past time previous to another past time, as in the following:

Gen. 2:2 — And he rested (a pa) on the seventh day from all the work which *he had made* (a prev pa).

A previous present is a present time which is previous to another present time, as in the following:

Isa. 1:4 — Ah, sinful nation . . . children dealing (a pre) corruptly! *They have forsaken* (a prev pre) Yahweh.

A previous future is a future time which is thought of as previous to another future time, as in the following:

I Sam. 20:22 — Go (a fut), for Yahweh *will have sent* (a prev fut) you.

A subsequent past is a past time which was subsequent to another past time, as in the following:

Jer. 52:7 — Then a breach was made (a pa) in the city, and all the men of war *proceeded to flee* (a sub pa).

A subsequent present is a present time which is subsequent to another present time, as in the following:

I Sam. 21:15; 21:14 in Eng — You begin to see (a pre) a man going mad. Wherefore do you *proceed to bring* (a sub pre) him unto me?

A subsequent future is a future time which will be subsequent to another future time, as in the following:

Isa. 10:3, 4 — And what will you do (a fut) for the day of visitation? . . . Without me they shall bow down (a fut) under the prisoners, and under the slain they *will proceed to fall* (a sub fut).

III

MOOD

Mood originally meant mind, feeling, or heart. It is used now to describe one's spirit, attitude, or temper. In grammar mood describes the subject's manner of feeling or thinking concerning the state of the verb.

The mood is indicative when the state is thought of as a fact; subjunctive when it is considered contrary-to-fact, potential, or optative; imperative when one commands the doing or acceptance of it.

The indicative mood, because it views that state as a fact, naturally accords with the nature of the perfect and of the participle. Any perfect standing alone, i.e., apart from the particles used to mark a contrary-to-fact idea, is indicative. Likewise, any participle standing alone is indicative. Imperfects may be either indicative or subjunctive, being indicative when the context shows that the author expected the state of the verb to be realized.

The subjunctive mood, because it views the state as unreal or uncertain, naturally accords with the nature of the imperfect. To indicate that an idea is possible, a simple imperfect is used, and the context alone is depended upon to show that it is a potential subjunctive. To indicate that a possibility is also the desire of the author, special forms of the imperfect are used; a special suffix or an internal vowel change is depended upon to show that they are optative subjunctives. The only way the subjunctive can use perfects or participles is by placing before them particles which indicate that a statement is contrary-to-fact. The combination uses their established nature to establish the unreality of the statement in which they appear.

The cohortative and the jussive belong to the same mood. Both express desire, urgency, i.e., an optative mood. Both appear with forms of the imperfect, the cohortative regularly with forms in the first person, and the jussive regularly with forms in the second or third person. The two supply what is known in English as optative subjunctives.

The cohortative is indicated by the addition of the letter *h* to the verb form or by a vowel change, and, when negative, by the use of the negative particle *'al*.

The jussive is indicated sometimes by the use of the negative particle *'al*, sometimes by a vowel change, and sometimes by the context alone.

The imperative is sometimes indicated by its own special form, sometimes by the use of an imperfect in the second person with the negative particle *lo'*, and sometimes by the context alone.

The special form of the imperative is used to express positive commands only (cf. Ex. 20:12).

The imperfect in the second person may also be used to express prohibitions (cf. Ex. 20:10).

The imperfect in the second person may also be used to express a positive command. In such a case the context alone is relied upon to indicate the imperative idea (cf. Ex. 20:9).

CONCLUSION: DISTINCTIVE TRANSLATIONS

When the three foregoing points of syntax have been determined, their combination furnishes a guide to the translation. In existing translations the lack of uniformity in the handling of these points causes a serious loss of clarity and vividness. Many have concluded that uniformity in the determination and translation of these points is impossible. Nevertheless, the present suggestions concerning them grow out of a belief that the Hebrew authors did work upon uniform principles in their use of them and that an attempt to regain the force of the original is worthy of the best of our efforts.

The table that follows suggests a distinctive translation for each combination of syntactical points.   Only active verbs in the active voice are used.   However, the parallels for stative verbs and for the passive forms of active verbs may be worked out easily.   These distinctive translations seek to express the essential idea in each combination in such a way that it may be clearly distinguished from all others.   The exact wording of the distinctive translations cannot be rigidly emulated in every translation, but the essential idea can be maintained.

The examples given in the treatment of varied developments following the table of distinctive translations are intended to demonstrate the possibility of maintaining the essential idea of the verb amid all the variations of translations.   The wording of existing translations, preferably that of the American Standard Version, is used wherever it appears to be true to the essential idea; but a new wording is offered where existing translations seem to fail to make that idea clear.   With each group of illustrations the combination of syntactical points is indicated so that comparison with the table of distinctive translations may be made.

A TABLE OF DISTINCTIVE TRANSLATIONS

STATE	TIME	MOOD	TRANSLATION
1. Com	Pa	Ind	He killed.
2. Com	Pre	Ind	He kills, he does kill.
3. Com	Fut	Ind	He shall kill.
4. Com	Prev pa	Ind	He had killed.
5. Com	Prev pre	Ind	He has killed.
6. Com	Prev fut	Ind	He will have killed. He shall have killed
7. Inc	Pa	Ind	He repeatedly killed.
8. Inc	Pre	Ind	He repeatedly kills.
9. Inc	Fut	Ind	He will repeatedly kill.
10. Inc	Sub pa	Ind	He began to kill. He proceeded to kill.
11. Inc	Sup pre	Ind	He begins to kill. He proceeds to kill.
12. Inc	Sub fut	Ind	He will begin to kill. He will proceed to kill.
13. Cont	Pa	Ind	He was killing.
14. Cont	Pre	Ind	He is killing.
15. Cont	Fut	Ind	He will be killing.
16. Com	Pa	Con subj	If he had killed.
17. Com	Fut	Con subj	Who can kill?
18. Inc	Fut	Pot subj	He could kill. He would kill. He should kill.
19. Inc	Fut	Opt subj (Coh)	I (or we) will kill. Let me (or us) kill. I am willing to kill.
20. Inc	Fut	Opt subj (Jus)	Do thou kill. Let him kill.
21. Inc	Fut	Imv (Imp)	Thou shalt kill.
22. Inc	Fut	Imv	Kill thou.
23. Inc	Fut	Imv & Jus	Kill thou—oh do kill!

Chapter Three

Indicative Perfects

All indicative perfects describe completed states. They are single, finished, and certain. In other words, a perfect looks at one thing, sees it as a whole, and thinks of it as certain.

The fact of fundamental importance is that a perfect is single. Whereas an imperfect may describe a state as the first in a series, implying a relation to others of its kind, a perfect pictures it alone, not bearing within itself any indication of relation to other states. There may be others, the context may indicate a relation, but a perfect does not link itself to another verb in any way. "Created" in Gen. 1:1 describes the one act of creation performed "in the beginning" and gives no hint concerning the other acts of creation.

(This view of the perfect is contrary to the generally accepted interpretation of the perfect when it is accompanied by the conjunction *waw*. According to Gesenius, Driver, Muller, Harper, and apparently all other authors who have dealt with the subject, the perfect with *waw* may receive the force of a frequentative imperfect. If so, Hebrew fails to maintain in its use of the perfect and imperfect a distinctive meaning for each, one that is always true to the fundamental nature of its own form. It is intended in this work to take issue with that kind of interpretation. In the treatment below of correlative perfects, further discussion of the matter will be found.)

The single state described by a perfect is also finished. An imperfect may describe the beginning of development of a state, but a perfect sees its conclusion and perfected character. The "was" of Gen. 1:2 asserts that the "waste and void" or unorganized state of original matter existed at the time it was created. A translation

35

like "came to be" would be contrary to the nature of the perfect. On the other hand, many imperfects are used in Gen. 1:3-19 to describe those developments through which law and order emerged in the material universe.

The single whole described by a perfect is also considered as certain. An imperfect may picture a state as possible or desired or expected, but a perfect sees it as actual, real, and sure. The "let us make" of Gen. 1:26 expresses God's desire that the formation of man should proceed, implying that it did not exist at the time of the speaking. The "he had made" of Gen. 1:31 refers to it as already accomplished.

It is helpful to note that each perfect bears all of these three general characteristics. Let us emphasize the *and* as we say that a perfect state is single, *and* finished, *and* certain.

In addition to these general characteristics, various groups of perfects manifest some characteristics peculiar to themselves. To facilitate study of these, the following classifications are suggested.

I

SIMPLE PERFECTS

The great majority of perfects are simple in *all* their relations, and it is this simplicity which distinguishes them from other perfects. While all perfects are simple in the sense of being singular, simple perfects are also uncomplicated by relationships indicated by the context. Some perfects are so related within the context as to show one of the following facts: (1) that their time is previous to another time; (2) that their state is characteristic of a life or period of time; (3) that the facts they describe are correlatives of another fact. Simple perfects, however, remain entirely unrelated to other verbs. They are uncomplicated within or without.

These simple perfects include both active and stative verbs. There is no difference between the two as far as the foregoing is concerned. The following examples, however, will reveal slight differences in other ways.

1. Simple Actions:

A simple action belongs to an exact point or period of time. A period, therefore, serves well as a graph for it (.).

    (1) A past time (Combination 1):

        Gen. 1:1 — In the beginning God *created* the heavens . . . .

The state is complete, for the verb is a perfect standing alone. The time is past, for it describes the beginning of creation. The mood is indicative, for it is part of a narrative. Translation should not involve difficulties here. AV, ASV, and RSV give it according to the accepted text. When MNT and AT amend this sentence, making it a time clause dependent on verse 2, they obscure the leading statement of a great story. Hebrew narrative under normal circumstances, i.e., when there is no context to indicate the contrary, begins with a perfect.

Syntactical summary: com-pa-ind (nar)

Gen. 6:9 — Noah *walked* with God.

The state is complete, for the verb is a perfect standing alone. It describes Noah's life as a whole, not at various times. The time is past, for it is the time of Noah. The mood is indicative, for it is part of a narrative. Translation is again a simple matter. AV, ASV, RSV, MNT, and AT, all agree in rendering it. MNT paraphrases the meaning of the verb but does not differ as to syntax.

Syntactical summary: com-pa-ind (nar)

Gen. 36:2 — Esau *took* his wives of the daughters of Canaan.

A frequentative imperfect could have been used, but the author's choice of a perfect indicates that he looked at the one fact of Esau's taking heathen wives, not the separate instances of such conduct. Translation is easy in this case also. AT paraphrases the meaning but is true to the syntax.

Syntactical summary: com-pa-ind (nar)

All the verbs above are narrative perfects. Being in past time where completeness is obvious, they exhibit plainly the normal characteristics of a perfect. It is helpful, therefore, to realize that past time is the most natural atmosphere for a perfect and that any appearance in another time needs to be carefully observed. Whenever a perfect appears in present or future time, it takes on a special significance.

(2) In present time (Combination 2):

II Sam. 24:23 — All this, O king, *does* Araunah *give* to the king.

The time is present, for these words are the conclusion of Araunah's offer to give (cf. 24:22), not a statement that he did give. David did not permit him to give. These facts are missed by AV but recognized by ASV, RSV, MNT, and AT. The mood is indicative, for Araunah is stating as positively as possible that so far as willingness can go he does give everything to David. Translation needs to bring out the emphasis of Araunah, and also to distinguish between such emphasis upon an isolated fact and the use of a perfect to mark a fact as characteristic of a life. The translation of RSV, MNT, and AT, because they lack emphatic auxiliaries, do not do this. Therefore, the translation of ASV is chosen, except that "doth" is changed to "does" according to a modern English trend.

Syntactical summary: com-pre-ind (em)

> I Kings 1:11 — Have you not heard that Adonijah . . .
> *does reign.*

Apparently we have here another simple present, as recognized by AV and ASV. MNT, AT, and RSV have substituted a previous present by paraphrasing the meaning of the verb. When we stick to its real meaning, it is an emphatic affirmation of the fact that Adonijah reigns which fits the context.

Syntactical summary: Com-pre-ind (em)

> Gen. 14:22 — I *do lift up* my hand to Yahweh.

The time appears to be present, despite the fact that AV, ASV, RSV, and AT have interpreted it as previous present. MNT interprets it as present. Both a past (I lifted up) and a previous present (I have lifted up) appear to be ruled out by the fact that the lifting up of the hand signified an oath, and there had been no occasion for it prior to the suggestion in 14:21 that Abram take the spoil for himself. That suggestion apparently provoked the oath then and there. The mood is indicative because Abram was affirming the taking of an oath. The translation needs to reflect the emphatic positiveness of Abram in taking this oath. As stated in 14:23, Abram's desire was to prevent the king of Sodom from saying, "I have made Abram rich." This desire evidently provoked his emphatic use of the perfect in affirming his oath. Accordingly, we use the emphatic auxiliary "do" to reflect the strength of his mood.

Syntactical summary: com-pre-ind (em)

> I Kings 1:35 — And him I *do appoint* to be prince.

The time appears to be present, because the verb describes actual installation and there had been no such act previously. The mood is indicative, for David was affirming the appointment as shown by 1:33-35a. The translation must needs make obvious the emphatic switch from an ordinary indicative imperfect in future time (1:35a) to this emphatic perfect in present time (1:35b); therefore, the emphatic auxiliary is used again.

Syntactical summary: com-pre-ind (em)

All verbs in this group may well be called emphatic perfects. The effect of any simple perfect in present time is emphatic, and it may be reflected in translation by the use of emphatic auxiliaries. They should be carefully distinguished from previous-present perfects and characteristic perfects, which are also in present time.

(3) In future time (Combination 3):

The effect of any simple perfect in future time is an emphasis upon the assurance felt by the speaker concerning the fulfilment of his words. In all cases there is unwavering assurance, but the reasons for that assurance vary. Further classification of these expressions is suggested as a means of helping us recognize these various reasons. Every such expression is a matter of unusual importance in Scripture, and we should not fail to recognize one when we meet it.

  a. Perfects of Confidence:

    Gen. 17:16 — And moreover *I will give* you a son of her.

    All translations recognize the assurance expressed by this perfect in future time, and they reflect it by the use of the auxiliary "will" with the first person.

Syntactical summary: com-fut-ind (con)

    Gen. 30:13 — The daughters *shall* surely *call* me blessed.

    AV, ASV, RSV, and MNT make no attempt to reflect the force of this perfect in future time. They handle it exactly as they handle an imperfect interpreted as a pure future. AT makes an attempt by introducing the adverb "certainly." No objection need be raised to this or similar adverbs. But why not add a simple step corresponding to the use of "will" with the first person, as seen in Gen. 17:16, and use the auxiliary "shall" with the second or third person?

Syntactical summary: com-fut-ind (con)

    Num. 17:27; 17:12 in Eng — We *will die,* we *will perish,* all of us *will perish.*

All translations put these verbs in the present. Apparently they interpret them as emphatic or characteristic perfects. Two separate statements in the verse following, however, show that the perishing and dying is viewed as future. That being true, the perfects that are used should be interpreted as perfects of confidence. They express the certainty the speakers felt about an event that was future to them. This sense of certainty arose from their own thinking, not from revelation. Perfects of certainty reflect both of these facts.

Syntactical summary: com-fut-ind (con)

The name perfect of confidence fits these verbs better than perfect of certainty, which has been generally used. The idea of certainty applies in some sense to all perfects in future time, but it does not distinguish one group from another. The basis of assurance in this group is self-assurance or confidence, no matter whether it be proper self-reliance or unwarranted cocksureness. God's assurance in Gen. 17:16 was of course warranted. Leah's in Genesis 30:13 was probably so, but that of the Israelites in Num. 17:27 was a case of jumping to conclusions. In all cases there is that feeling of certainty that grows out of confidence on the part of the speaker, but there may be no certainty otherwise concerning fulfilment of the speaker's words.

b. Prophetic Perfects:

Isa. 11:8 — And upon the den of an adder a weaned child *shall put* his hand.

AV, ASV, and RSV have used "shall" here. "Shall" in such cases is used also by W. R. Harper.[1] MNT uses a paraphrase which gives no place for either "shall" or "will," thus obscuring one of the most prominent features of the language. AT uses "will," and in doing so it apparently develops an inconsistency in its own usage. From 10:33 to this verse it interprets a series of perfects with *waw* as receiving the force of a pure future imperfect in third person as found in 10:33 and uses "will" with each one. Since it accepts "will" as the characteristic for the future imperfects and for perfects linked to it by *waw*, what can there be even in its own premises to justify the handling of a perfect sepa-

---

1. W. R. Harper, *Elements of Hebrew Syntax* (New York: Charles Scribner's Sons, 1888), p. 57.

rated from *waw* as though it were another imperfect? Such failures to maintain the distinctions of the Hebrew ought to arouse us to see the urgent need of adopting methods of translation that will maintain those distinctions. Prophetic perfects were used by the prophets with fine discrimination, to give climactic touches of power to their perorations, and we are throwing away jewels of prophetic teaching when we allow the muddy waters of indistinct translations to obscure them.

Syntactical summary: com-fut-ind (pro)

Isa. 9:5; 9:6 in Eng — For to us a child *shall be born, a son *shall be given* to us.

All the translations have used present time here: AV, ASV, RSV, and AT the simple present, MNT a previous present. This is not done because they consider these verbs as describing the actual present. Instead they are applying an interpretation which is stated by S. R. Driver as follows: ". . . continually the series of perfects is interspersed with the simple future forms, as the prophet shifts his point of view, at one moment contemplating the events he is describing from the *real standpoint* of the present, at another moment looking back upon them as accomplished and done and so viewing them from an *ideal position* in the future."[2] Such supposed shifting of viewpoint is very confusing, even to the student of the Hebrew text. It leaves the reader of the English hopelessly lost. Moreover, this supposition is not necessary. Adoption of "shall" as a characteristic of the perfect in second or third person and in future time would mark it clearly as future, as distinguished from the pure future imperfect using "will," and as indicating the dramatic certainty of the prophetic perfect.

Syntactical summary: com-fut-ind (pro)

Num. 24:17 — There *shall come forth* a star out of Jacob.

Again the "shall come" of AV, ASV, and RSV is clear, and the "has come" of MNT and AT is confusing. The reference is unquestionably to the future, as shown by the first part of the verse. Then let that reference be clear and strong.

2. S. R. Driver, *A Treatise on the Use of the Tenses in Hebrew* (3rd ed.; Oxford: The Clarendon Press, 1892), p. 19.

Syntactical summary: com-fut-ind (pro)
Other examples appear in Isa. 5:13; 8:8; 9:1; 10:28; 28:2; 53:12; Hos. 4:6; Amos 5:2; Ps. 67:7; 110:5.

The basis for assurance in these cases is a revelation from God on one hand and faith on the other. This faith is always warranted because it is based on God. Though the prophet prove to be unworthy, as did Balaam, the speaker of Num. 24:17, the prophetic word never will prove unworthy, for its author and finisher is God.

If a question arises as to whether a verb be a perfect of confidence (word of the author) or a prophetic perfect (word received by the author from God), the determinative question must be, Does the Scripture passage represent it as a word received from God? This question need not trouble us greatly in translation, for we translate the same way in both cases; but it helps to clarify the meaning of these idioms.

The faith expressed in these perfects is identified with the prophets, and the name prophetic perfect fits them well.

It is very important to note that all perfects of confidence and prophetic perfects appear apart from conjunctions. This fact sharply distinguishes them from the correlative perfects which will be described later.

It is also very important to observe that the auxiliary of the verb, the "shall" or the "will," is the reverse of the one ordinarily used. We ought to utilize every means at our command to retain in our translations the force of these peculiarly important idioms, and there appears to be no way in English to do this except through rigid observance of the distinctions between "shall" and "will." With the first person "will" is used here to indicate the positiveness of these perfects, because "shall" in these cases would make a mild statement. With the second and third persons "shall" is used here to indicate the positiveness of these perfects, because "will" in these cases would make a mild statement.

In addition to making it possible for a discerning reader of the English text, even though he lack a knowledge of Hebrew, to take note of prophetic perfects, this method of translation would eliminate from English translations much confusing fluctuation in the handling of the English future tense. Any extensive comparison of AV, ERV, ASV, RSV, MNT, and AT will reveal the fact that this fluctuation is widespread.

It is doubtless due in large measure to the problems involved
in interpreting the so-called *waw* consecutive with perfects.
These cannot be dealt with until we have gone further in
our study of perfects and of the conjunction *waw*. We may
observe even here, however, that the suggestions made
above are in accord with the highest literary standards.
George O. Curme says, concerning a pure future in English:
"Shall in the first person, singular and plural, is the standard
usage in England, though not uniformly observed, and is
still the preferred form in the higher grades of literary language in America, though now not so uniformly used as it
once was."[3]   Accordingly, he says concerning the modal use
of "shall" in the second and third persons: "As a modal
auxiliary it indicates the will of someone other than its
subject, representing its subject as standing under the will of
another who commands him, promises or assures him something, wishes something to be arranged to suit him, threatens
him, resolves to do something for his benefit or injury, or
it represents the speaker as determined to bring something
about or prevent it. . . .   It represents the speaker as pro-
claiming the will of God or destiny in a prophetic or oracular
announcement of something that shall take place."[4]

2. Simple states:

Some stative verbs describe intellectual, emotional, or volitional
states: know, remember, hate, love, refuse, trust, and rejoice.
Some of them describe pure states of being: be righteous, be high,
be full, be old, be beautiful, be weary, and be great.   In all cases
there is no real action, only a condition of body, mind, or spirit.

A simple state is like a simple action in that it stands as a unit,
singular, finished, and certain.   It is different, however, in that it
is indefinitely extended beyond the time of completion.   One
knows and keeps on knowing.   The fitting graph is a short line
(————).

   (1) In past time (Combination 1):
   Gen. 40:23 — But the chief butler *remembered* not.
   Ex. 1:7 — And the children of Israel *were fruitful*.

3. George O. Curme, *A Grammar of the English Language* (Boston:
D. C. Heath and Company, 1935), III, p. 363.
   4. *Ibid.*, pp. 364, 365.

Ps. 31:15; 31:14 in Eng — But I *trusted* in Thee, O Yahweh.

Syntactical summary: com-pa-ind (nar)

These are narrative perfects as truly as are the simple active verbs in past time.

(2) In present time (Combination 2):

Ex. 3:19 — And as for me I *indeed know*.

Job 34:5 — I *am surely righteous*.

Ps. 31:7; 31:6 in Eng — But as for me in Yahweh *do I trust*.

Syntactical summary: com-pre-ind (em)

These are emphatic perfects. The use of adverbs and auxiliaries to bring out the emphatic force in the English needs to be carefully observed.

(3) In future time (Combination 3):

Isa. 11:9 — For the earth *shall be full* of the knowledge of Yahweh.

Isa. 15:9 — For the waters of Dimon *shall be full* of blood.

Isa. 53:10 — And Yahweh *shall be pleased* with the bruising of him.

Syntactical summary: com-fut-ind (pro)

These are prophetic perfects. Again "shall" with the third person is used to indicate that the state described is determined and absolutely certain.

II

PREVIOUS PERFECTS

One of the complications into which a perfect is brought by its context is that of previous completion. When it is written in Gen. 2:2, "And he rested on the seventh day from all his work which he had done," it is evident that God's work was completed before he rested. The fact that the state described is previous to another distinguishes a large group of verbs and gives occasion for the name previous perfect.

There is a combination of active and stative ideas always associated with a previous perfect. From Gen. 2:2 it is evident that the state resulting from God's work continued until he began to rest. The graph that fits this situation is a horizontal line

extended up to a perpendicular line representing the point of time
it precedes (————————⌐).

   (1) In past time (Combination 4):
      Gen. 2:8 — And he put there the man whom *he had
      formed.*
      I Sam. 28:20 — And there was no strength in him, for
      he had not eaten bread.
      I Kings 7:8 — Solomon made also a house for Pharaoh's
      daughter whom *he had taken* to wife.
   All translations agree here.

Syntactical summary: com-pa-ind (prev)

   (2) In present time (Combination 5):
      Isa. 1:3-4 — Israel does not know . . . they *have forsaken*
      Yahweh.
      Gen. 32:11; 32:10 in Eng — I am not worthy of the least
      of all the loving-kindnesses which thou *hast done* for
      thy servant.
      I Sam. 12:3 — Here I am: witness against me . . . whose
      ox *have I taken*?
   Again all translations agree.

Syntactical summary: com-pre-ind (prev)

   (3) In future time (Combination 6):
      Isa. 4:3-4 — And it shall come to pass that he that is
      left in Zion . . . will be called holy, . . . when the
      Lord *shall have washed away* the filth of the daughters
      of Zion.
   AV, ASV, and RSV use "shall have" here, and this previous
perfect in future time is clearly distinguished by it.   When
MNT and AT shift back to a previous present, they muddle
the question of time in the same way they do when translating
prophetic perfects.

Syntactical summary: com-fut-ind (prev)

      II Sam. 5:24 — And let it be . . . that then you will bestir
      yourself; for then Yahweh *shall have gone forth* before
      you . . . .
   AV appears to have interpreted this as a prophetic perfect,
disregarding the previous relation.   ASV and AT shift to present time, RSV to previous present time.   Only MNT gives it
as a previous future.   It uses "will have" instead of "shall have";
but the difference between these two is not great, and it seems

reasonable to accept either in translating previous relation in future time. "Shall" makes the statement a prophetic declaration, "will" makes it a simple affirmation, and it is impossible when previous relationship exists to tell how the author intended it.

Syntactical summary: com-fut-ind (prev)

> I Sam. 14:10 — Then we will go up, for Yahweh *shall have put* them in our hand.

AV, ASV, RSV, and AT use the previous present, and MNT the simple present. Yet their going up is of course future, and the time of Yahweh's putting their enemies into their hand is related to that. Putting into their hand refers to Yahweh's answer to their prayer, his overruling their test so as to give a sign of his will; and that answer had not been given at the moment Jonathan spoke.

Syntactical summary: com-fut-ind (prev)

All previous states are described by perfects, and all subsequent ones by imperfects. Thus it appears that the name previous perfect is fitting because of the obvious contrast with the subsequent nature of those imperfects usually called Progressives.

III

CHARACTERISTIC PERFECTS

Another complication into which a perfect is occasionally brought by its context is that of characteristic or typical significance. A single act or state is made to typify the character of a person or thing. This relation gives occasion for the name characteristic perfect.

When it is said in Isa. 1:3, "An ox knows his master . . . , Israel does not know," we understand that recognition of his master is a distinguishing trait or characteristic of an ox but not of Israel. We know this because the whole chapter is devoted to a description of the moral character of Israel. When the contrast between an ox and Israel is drawn in the midst of this characterization of Israel, it is obvious that Isaiah is characterizing both, telling not merely what they know at some particular moment, but what kind of knowledge distinguishes one from the other.

The fitting graph for this characteristic perfect is a period within a circle, a single act or state corresponding to a larger but similar sphere (⊙).

Job 7:9 — A cloud *is temporary* and proceeds to go away.

Isa. 40:7 — Grass *withers,* a flower *fades.*

Ps. 1:1 — Blessed is the man who *walks* not in the counsel of the wicked, and in the way of the sinners he *stands* not, and in the seat of the scoffers he *sits* not.

In Job 7:9 and Isa. 40:7 all translations agree, giving clear recognition to this kind of perfect. Ps. 1:1 is handled the same way in AV, ASV, and RSV, but MNT gives its verbs what appears to be an emphatic interpretation, and AT makes them previous presents. Emphasis must be admitted as a possible interpretation, but there is no clear ground for a previous relation. In many cases, as in Ps. 119:113, the possibility of more than one interpretation must be admitted, and each interpreter left to his choice.

All characteristic perfects appear to be in present time. Their extended application to a sphere of life or being accords with such usage, their present being a broad unrestricted present without any specific limitations as to time. In other words, that which is asserted to be true now is generally true of the subject.

Syntactical summary: com-pre-ind (ch)

The three perfects in present time need to be clearly distinguished. These three kinds are: (1) emphatic; (2) previous; (3) characteristic. The emphatic ones stress the fact that a certain state does exist; the previous ones indicate that the state occurred before another; and the characteristic ones make the state typical of some life or thing. In translation the emphatic ones may be marked by emphatic auxiliaries or adverbs; the previous ones by the auxiliaries "had," "has" (or have), and "shall have" accompanying the participle; and the characteristic ones by absence of these auxiliaries.

IV

CORRELATIVE PERFECTS

Another complication for a perfect develops when it is linked by the conjunction *waw* to a preceding expression so as to indicate a correlative relationship. As the word "father" and the word "son" imply each other, or as a whole and its parts imply each other, so a perfect with *waw* attached and its antecedent imply each other. This relationship is correlative and gives occasion for the name correlative perfect.

A circle, representing the antecedent, divided into segments, which are its correlatives, will furnish a graph (⊕).

The visible mark of correlative perfects is their immediate connection with the conjunction. It is always attached to them, but never to other perfects.

The translation of correlative perfects need not differ from that of other perfects except for the immediate connection with the conjunction. Scrupulous care should be exercised to maintain the connection with correlatives and to avoid it with others. Sometimes it may be necessary to let the subject come between the conjunction and verb in order to make a natural sentence in English, but the close connection between conjunction and verb ought to be made as obvious as possible in all cases.

Students need to realize that the interpretation of the conjunction *waw* is a matter of far-reaching significance in Hebrew. A separate study of it will be undertaken after all verb forms have been studied and in connection with sentence structure.

In each case there are two verbs to be considered: the perfect with *waw,* and whatever verb precedes it, which will be called its antecedent. In Gen. 2:10, for instance, "was as it were four heads" represents the perfect with *waw,* and "began to be divided" represents its antecedent.

When these two verbs are alike, both being perfects, all translators agree in making them co-ordinate. Inasmuch as correlation includes co-ordination, differing from ordinary co-ordination merely in the fact that its co-ordination is inherent and permanent, the translation works out well in all cases.

When the two verbs are different, however, translations differ in all sorts of ways. In Gen. 2:10, where the antecedent is an imperfect, AV, ASV, and RSV translate that imperfect like a perfect and the perfect with *waw* like an imperfect, while MNT and AT avoid the problem by paraphrasing in ways that disregard the original text. In Deut. 11:10, where the antecedent is also an imperfect, AV, ASV, RSV, and MNT translate both as perfects, while AT translates both as imperfects. And this confusion appears in the very places where the old theory of *waw* consecutive with the perfect is supposed to apply regularly, i.e., in narratives begun with an imperfect and continued by perfects with *waw.* (Cf. Pars. 49-3 and Par. 112 of *Gesenius' Hebrew*

Grammar; Chapter VII of *The Use of the Tenses in Hebrew* by S. R. Driver; pp. 17ff. of *Hebrew Syntax* by August Muller; Par. 25 of *Elements of Hebrew Syntax* by W. R. Harper.)

The explanation of perfects with *waw* as correlatives offers one explanation for all of them and a way out of this confusion in translation. According to it, correlative perfects may follow any kind of antecedent and yet be translated as perfects, the correlative relation being indicated by the attachment of the perfect to the conjunction.

1. In past time (Combination 1):

Gen. 2:10 — And a river was going out from Eden, . . . and from there it began to be divided *and was as it were four heads* (lit, *for four heads*).

As the delta land of the garden of Eden made the river divide, its four divisions were like the separate headwaters of a great stream. "Began to be divided" and "was as it were four heads" are different descriptions of the same thing.

Josh. 6:8, 9 — Then it proceeded to be so, that . . . seven priests passed over, bearing seven rams' horns as trumpets before Yahweh, *and they blew* upon the trumpets. The armed men were going before the priests who blew upon the trumpets, and the rear portion [of the priests] was going after the ark, going on steadily and blowing continuously.

These two verses together make it quite obvious that the passing over did not occur separately from the blowing of the trumpets. The passing over and the blowing were two phases of one general movement. Thus the perfect "and they blew" at the end of 6:8 furnishes an excellent example of a correlative perfect. The absence of sequence is obvious. The inseparable relation of the two actions as parts of one general movement, actions that combined the military and the religious warning to the enemy, is likewise clear.

Deut. 2:30 — Yahweh your God hardened his spirit *and made strong* his heart.

Hardening and making strong (or obstinate) are obviously different descriptions of the same thing. Thus they are correlative ideas.

Deut. 11:10 — Where you were accustomed to sow your seed, *and you watered* with your foot as the garden of herbs.

Watering with the foot is a part of the process of sowing seed, as it is done in an irrigated land. A toe is used to break a ridge and let water from an adjoining furrow flow over the seed that has just been dropped. These likewise are correlative ideas.

Ps. 27:2 — They stumbled *and fell.*

Stumbling and falling are parts of such a downfall or destruction of enemies as the context contemplates. Being parts of the same whole, they too are correlative ideas.

In past time correlative perfects are translated like narrative perfects. Their connection with the conjunction, however, distinguishes them, for Hebrew usage does not permit ordinary narrative perfects to be linked together by *waw.*

Syntactical summary: com-pa-ind (cor)

2. In present time (Combination 2 or 3):

Isa. 1:2 — Children I have made great *and have exalted.*

Hos. 4:3 — The land mourns continually, *and is faint* every inhabitant of it.

Jer. 12:3 — And thou, O Yahweh, dost know me, thou seest me continually, *and dost test me.*

Syntactical Summary: com-pa-ind (cor)

In other translations the same sort of confusion is found as was seen above. In Isa. 1:2 there is agreement, for the verbs are both perfects. In Hos. 4:3, where the antecedent is an imperfect, AV and ARV treat both as prophetic perfects, while MNT, AT, and RSV put both in present time. In Jer. 12:3, where the antecedent is also an imperfect, AV treats both like previous perfects, while ASV, RSV, and AT apparently, but not clearly, treat both as imperfects, and MNT paraphrases. In all three cases the two verbs describe parts of the same thing and thus are correlated.

As the above examples show, correlatives in present time may be translated like a previous present perfect, a characteristic perfect, or an emphatic perfect. Still they are distinguished by the connection with *waw,* for Hebrew usage does not permit any other perfect to be linked with *waw.*

3. In future time (Combination 3):

Gen. 17:20 — Behold, I will bless him (pf of con), yea *I will make him fruitful,* and *I will multiply him* exceedingly.

Gen. 40:13 — Within three days Pharaoh will lift up your head *and shall restore you* to your office, *and you shall put* the cup of Pharaoh into his hand.

Isa. 2:2 — The house of Yahweh will be established at the head of the mountains, *and shall be exalted* above hills, *and shall flow* to it all the nations.

Ex. 19:10-13 — *Go* to the people, *and you shall sanctify* them . . . *and they shall wash* their garments, *and they shall be ready* . . . *and you shall set* bounds.

Syntactical summary: com-fut-ind (cor)

The translations often put a terrific strain on subjective judgment in deciding what interpretations to give to the perfects with *waw*. In Gen. 17:20, where the antecedent is another perfect, they are made co-ordinate; and the translation works out well. In Gen. 40:13 and Isa. 2:2, where the antecedents are imperfects, they are made imperfects. In Ex. 19:10-13, where the antecedent is an imperative, two are made imperatives, but one is made a jussive imperfect, and another is made a potential subjunctive. In other words, the imperative antecedent is considered, for the purpose of the old theory, the equivalent of an imperfect in its effect on the perfects that follow; then the *waw* with the perfects is supposed to give to the perfects the force of an imperfect, but that imperfect may be any kind of imperfect; and the translator switches around from one to another with no apparent guidance other than his own subjective judgment. This kind of thing is done quite frequently. If the translations always made these perfects to receive the force of their antecedents, at least the application of their theory would be clear. But alas! the fact that they do so most of the time and the results in those instances happen to be what we are accustomed to in English gives a plausibility to their theory that lulls us into forgetting the strange logic of it. When we take time, however, to examine the many instances in which it fails to lead to any justifiable interpretation of the text, we are faced with the conclusion that it is inadequate.

In AT many efforts to attain more distinctive translations have been made, and some of them appear here. In all cases the antecedents and their attached perfects are kept in the same time. In Gen. 17:20, the prophetic perfect used as an antecedent is put in future time and marked by an emphatic adverb. In Isa. 2:2, the imperfect used as an antecedent is clearly treated as an imperfect. These efforts are a tremendous improvement over many unjustified paraphrases by which MNT avoided the problems which all students of the subject knew to exist in previous works. While AT has not escaped the confusion entirely, it has at least tried to stick to the text and to interpret it.

The correlative relations in these examples appear as follows: in Gen. 17:20, making fruitful and multiplying are parts of the blessing; in Gen. 40:13, restoration to office and performance of one of its functions by putting Pharaoh's cup in his hand are parts of the lifting up of the chief butler's head; in Isa. 2:2, exaltation above hills (little powers) and the coming of the nations like a stream are parts of the same great restoration of Israel to which belongs establishment at the head of the mountains (big powers); and in Ex. 19:10-13, Moses' sanctifying the people, their washing their garments, their getting ready, and Moses' setting of bounds are all details of the situation which Moses was expected to put in order, thus being correlated in the mind of the speaker with the command to go.

The translations of these correlatives may be handled exactly like perfects of confidence and prophetic perfects, except for the connection with the conjunction.

It is helpful to observe that these perfects with *waw* are very common in future time. At some points in the future they pile up, any number being used in a series. After imperatives the details of the command are customarily given by them. Also they are used constantly in lengthy descriptions of the future. In prophetic utterances several chapters may be tied together by them. This frequent use in future time is in sharp contrast with a decidedly infrequent use in past and present time. Thus their frequent use in future time becomes a feature of the language, that verb whose natural element is the past being shifted to the future when attached to the conjunction.

A corresponding peculiarity of the imperfect must be kept in mind while studying this situation. Whereas the natural element of the imperfect is future time, when attached to *waw* consecutive it appears almost always in the past.

Examining all these evidences, we realize that these idioms are very peculiar, very closely related to each other, and very important.

The freedom with which we link English perfects in past time after this fashion, "They ran and they skipped and they played," and English imperfects in future time after this fashion, "They will run and skip and play," is that which makes the Hebrew idiom so strange to us. Hebrew never uses either of these ways of expression. Moreover, when we take into account the fact that "the other Semitic languages do not exhibit this peculiarity, excepting occasionally the Phoenician, the most closely related to Hebrew, and of course the Moabitish dialect of the *Mesa* inscription, which is practically identical with Old Hebrew,"[5] we know that probably we must look to Biblical Hebrew alone for evidence bearing on an explanation.

This shift of both perfects and imperfects to the natural time of the other when they are attached to certain forms of *waw* indicates that the fundamental characteristics of each pertain to the state represented and in no sense to time. In these relations, therefore, we have excellent oportunity for comparison and marking essential distinctions.

The importance of these idioms in Hebrew is indicated by the fact that few passages omit the use of one or the other. Moreover, the meaning of highly important passages depends upon their interpretation. Their use is so important as to color more or less the whole language.

Therefore, let the foregoing observations concerning the nature of the Hebrew perfect be accepted as evidence to be weighed in connection with the nature of the imperfect and the various forms of the conjunction *waw*. As tentative steps in this study the following suggestions may be kept in mind:

1. The correlative nature of the perfect with *waw* fitted it for the account of details in extended descriptions of the future. When looking into the future, it is impossible for human understanding to grasp much of the sequence of things. This remains true even when the mind of man is illumined by the light of prophecy. One may become conscious of many circumstances of revealed truths, yet remain unaware of their temporal and logical order, seeing only their inherent connections with some central fact. It is understandable, therefore, that prophecy should multiply correlative perfects and minimize consecutive imperfects.

5. E. Kautzsch, *Gesenius' Hebrew Grammar* (28th ed.; Oxford; The Clarendon Press, 1910), p. 132.

2. The progressive nature of the imperfect with *waw* consecutive fitted it for tracing the sequences of history.   When telling stories and narrating history, human interest usually looks for chains of development which lead steadily onward to a goal.   Repetitions and details may be added when wanted, but the times when they are wanted are comparatively few.   It is understandable, therefore, that all narratives should multiply consecutive imperfects and minimize correlative perfects.

A SUMMARY OF INDICATIVE PERFECTS AND IMPERFECTS

Perfects (Single and finished and certain)		Imperfects (Partial)	
Name and Graph	*Distinctive Features*	*Name and Graph*	*Distinctive Features*
1. Simple	Unrelated	1. Frequentative	Part of a series
2. Previous ⌐	Effective up to another time	2. Progressive or Subsequent ⌐	Developing from another time
3. Characteristic ⊙	Typical of an individual	3. Characteristic ⊙	Typical of a group
4. Correlative ⊕	Coexistent and related logically by inherent and permanent co-ordination	4. Consecutive }}}}	Successive and linked by temporal or logical sequence

Chapter Four

Indicative Imperfects

All imperfects represent incomplete states. They are either repeated (fre), or developing (pro), or contingent (subj). In other words, they are either part of a series, or partially developed, or partially assured. In all cases they are partial in some sense, i.e., incomplete.

The state described by an imperfect is partial when it is frequentative, because it is part of a series of repetitions of the same act or condition. No one of these repetitions is seen as established and abiding. When Ps. 1:2 says, "And in his law he meditates day and night," the imperfect verb alone expresses the idea that the man meditates frequently. The words "day and night" carry out this idea more explicitly. The repeated meditations may produce development, but no one is seen as producing a fixed and permanent state of meditation such as a perfect would represent.

The state described by an imperfect is partial when it is progressive, because the progress described is only a part of its total development. One act or condition is described, but it is also true that only a part of it is described. In Ex. 15:1 such an imperfect, standing alone, suddenly appears in a historical account characterized by narrative perfects and imperfects with *waw* consecutive. If we translate after the fashion of the AV, saying, "Then sang Moses," we show utter disregard for the introduction of this imperfect apart from *waw* consecutive. W. R. Harper caught the force of it when he translated it thus, "Then Moses . . . proceeded to sing."[1]

1. W. R. Harper, *Elements of Hebrew Syntax* (New York: Charles Scribner's Sons, 1888, p. 59.

The state described by an imperfect is partial when it is subjunctive, because the assurance of its fulfillment is contingent upon the fulfilment of other matters. A possibility is indicated but not a certainty. Gen. 4:7, as translated by Moffatt, "Yet you ought to master it," indicates that it is possible for Cain to master sin but not certain that he will.

It is helpful to note that each imperfect bears only one of these three general characteristics. Let us emphasize the *or* as we say that an imperfect is frequentative *or* progressive *or* subjunctive.

To facilitate further study of these characteristics, the following classifications are suggested. We include here only the indicative ones, both frequentatives and progressives.

I

FREQUENTATIVE IMPERFECTS

The distinctive feature of frequentative imperfects is repetition. The fitting graph will be a series of dots, representing a repeated action, or a series of short lines, representing a repeated state (. . . . or - - - -). No effort will be made, in citing examples, to separate active and stative verbs.

Translation of this idea of repetition into English cannot as a rule be accomplished by English verbs standing alone. Some sort of adverbial modifier must be added. If the Hebrew text does not provide one like the "day and night" of Ps. 1:2, it is necessary to add to the English verb an adverb like frequently, repeatedly, regularly, customarily, habitually, or always. A paraphrase that says one is accustomed to do so and so has the same effect.

1. In past time (Combination 7):
    I Sam. 1:7 — And so he *did regularly year by year.* (Or) And so he *was accustomed to do year by year.*
    Judg. 21:25 — Each man *was accustomed to do* that which was right in his own eyes.
    Judg. 14:10 — For this the young men *were accustomed to do.*
    Ps. 55:15; 55:14 in Eng — We *were accustomed to take sweet* counsel together; in the house of God *we were accustomed to walk* in a throng.
Syntactical summary: inc-pa-ind (fre)
    This interpretation has been coming into the translations

gradually. AV and ASV have it only in Judg. 14:10; MNT in
I Sam. 1:7 and Judg. 14:10; AT in Judg. 21:25 and 14:10;
RSV in I Sam. 1:7; Judg. 14:10; Ps. 55:14a.

2. In present time (Combination 8):
   I Sam. 16:7 — For man *is accustomed to consider* according
   to the eyes, but God *is accustomed to consider* according to
   the heart.
   Isa. 1:11 — For what to me is the multitude of your sacrifices?
   constantly says Yahweh.
   Prov. 8:17 — As for me, the one who loves me I *always
   love,* and the one who diligently seeks me *always finds* me.

Syntactical summary: inc-pre-ind (fre)

The translations put nearly all of these verbs in present time,
but they make no distinction between them and characteristic or
emphatic perfects. The adverbs are needed to mark that distinction.

3. In future time (Combination 9):
   Ex. 4:16 — He *will be* to you for a mouth.
   Gen. 24:19 — I *shall draw* water for your camels.
   Hos. 14:5, 14:4 in Eng — I *shall heal* . . . I *shall love* them
   freely. (Or) I *shall always love* them freely.

Syntactical summary: inc-fut-ind (fre)

Through some unexplained influence all translations have been
led to put a modal interpretation on these verbs like a jussive
of decree or cohortative of determination. Yet outward signs
of the jussive or cohortative are lacking, and there appears
to be nothing in the contexts to require such interpretation. One
can see reasons why the authors might have used a jussive or
cohortative, but when evidence of the use of either of these comes
from the context alone, it ought to be decisive.

In future time the use of adverbs to bring out the frequentative
force is not so urgent as in other times. Some form of incomplete-
ness is obvious in any simple future statement. Whether that in-
completeness be due to a frequentative or a progressive idea can
be judged from the context. The only distinction that will matter
greatly will be that between perfects and imperfects in future time,
and it can be handled by strict observance of the suggestions concerning "shall" and "will." We may exercise our choice, therefore,

concerning the use of adverbs according to our judgment as to
what makes the smoothest and most effective translation.

II
Progressive Imperfects

The distinctive feature of progressive imperfects is development
or progress. Whereas frequentatives indicate repeated occurrences,
progressives describe a single occurrence while in progress.
Whereas perfects describe one thing as complete, progressives
describe one thing as being in a process of development.

In all cases of progress there is a starting point, for progress is
a movement onward from some point. Even when the point
of departure is not specified, it is understood to exist. With progressives in past time it is usually obvious. With those in
present and future time it is frequently obscure, yet it must
be taken for granted. Therefore, there is always a double reference to time, and the time of the verb is always subsequent to
another time mentioned or implied by the context. For this
reason progressives might fittingly be called subsequent imperfects. The fitting graph is a horizontal line, representing the act
or condition described, proceeding away from a perpendicular
line, which represents the time from which is proceeds (⌞▬▬▬).

The development of progressives, like the repetition of frequentatives, cannot as a rule be represented by the corresponding
English verbs standing alone. If their progress is in beginning, its
incipiency can be expressed by a combination of "begin" with
the infinitive of the English verb. If mere progress without reference to its beginning is indicated, the progressive force may be
expressed by a combination of "proceed" with the infinitive of
the English verb.

1. In past time (Combination 10):
   Judg. 2:1 — I *proceeded to bring* you up from Egypt.
   I Kings 3:16 — Then *proceeded to come* two women, harlots,
   to the king.
   I Kings 8:1 — Then Solomon *proceeded to assemble* the
   elders of Israel.
Syntactical summary: inc-pa-ind (prog)

No recognition has been given these imperfects in past time
by the translations. Nevertheless, they stand out in the midst

of historical narratives as clearly as the one pointed out by W. R. Harper in Ex. 15:1. They mark the fact that development started at a certain time, growing out of a situation just described. Thus the coming of the women of I Kings 3:16 happened immediately after God's promise to give Solomon wisdom. Their case came as a test and proof of his wisdom, and we miss part of the significance of this passage if we fail to see that.

2. In present time (Combination 11):

I Sam. 21:15; 21:14 in Eng — Behold you *begin to see a* man going crazy; wherefore do you *proceed to bring* him to me.

Num. 24:17 — I *begin to see* him but not now: I *begin to behold* him but not near.

Jer. 6:4 — The day has turned, and the shadows of evening *begin to lengthen.*

Syntactical summary: inc-pre-ind (prog or inc-prog)

Perhaps there is no profit in continuing to point out the vagaries of translations in each case. Our main purpose is to seek consistency for our own translation, and we may do so here from the basis of our previous definitions.

Ordinary progressives, those whose beginnings are not definitely marked by the context, and incipient progressives, those whose beginnings are definitely marked, are left in one category because their nature is essentially the same. Both are characterized by progress.

3. In future time (Combination 12):

Ex. 9:5 — Tomorrow Yahweh *will do* this thing. (Or) Tomorrow Yahweh *will proceed to do* this thing.

I Sam. 10:5 — After that you *will come* to the hill of God. (Or) After that you *will go on* to the hill of God.

I Sam. 20:21 — And, behold, I *shall send* the lad.

Syntactical summary: inc-fut-ind (prog)

In future time the need for the addition of auxiliaries like begin and proceed to bring out the progressive force is not nearly so strong. When it is said in I Sam. 24:21, "I know that you will surely be king," we understand this as meaning: "I know that you will surely become (or proceed to be) king." These verbs furnish the pure futures of English more naturally than any others, and as a rule it is doubtless well to let them be stated as simply as possible.

III

Characteristic Imperfects

Now and then the frequentative force of an imperfect is used to characterize an individual as a member of a group or species. Whereas a characteristic perfect designates a state which is typical of the whole life or character of an individual, a characteristic imperfect designates a state which marks one as a member of a certain group, because it is repeated in each member of that group. When Isa. 51:12 speaks of "a man that dies," it uses a word for man that means a mortal being, and the verb "dies" indicates that all mortals die. A graph may be made by making a circle, representing the characteristic act or condition, and enclosing a series of dots, which represent the members of the group. (⊛)

Gen. 49:27 — A wolf that *ravens*.

Isa. 62:1 — A lamp that *burns*.

Ps. 17:12 — A lion that *is greedy* of his prey.

Syntactical summary: inc-pre-ind (ch)

In translation a characteristic imperfect can hardly be distinguished from a characteristic perfect without resorting to cumbersome paraphrase. Both appear only in present time, and both need to be distinguished from emphatic perfects by avoiding emphatic auxiliaries. It appears best, therefore, to make no difference in the translation of the verbs themselves, leaving the reader to detect the imperfects by the fact that their subjects are typical of groups rather than isolated individuals. There are only a very few clear cases of the characteristic imperfect, and all of them appear in relative clauses introduced by "that"; so the problem of recognizing them is a small one after all.

IV

Consecutive Imperfects

Progressive imperfects are very frequently linked together so as to form a chain of sequences. A special form of the conjunction "and," a *waw* with *pathah* followed by *daghesh-forte*, is used with each verb in such a chain. This is the only use made of this special conjunction; so it appears to have been intended to mark the consecutive relationship of these imperfects. The name *"waw* consecutive" has been widely used for this conjunction and is quite appropriate. Likewise, the word "consecutive" may aptly be used to describe the imperfect which always accompanies a *waw* consecutive.

Occasionally a frequentative imperfect is introduced into the chains of progressive imperfects in the same way as a progressive. The frequentative bears no outward mark to distinguish it from the progressives. It depends upon its context or other sources bearing upon its context for evidences concerning its force as a frequentative. If there is evidence that its action or state was repeated, it is a frequentative. An example appears in Gen. 5:4 (Cf. discussion under 1. below). If there is evidence that the verb's action or state occurred only once, the verb is a progressive. An example appears in Gen. 5:3 (Cf. discussion under 1. below). If there is no clear evidence, it is probably best to consider the verb progressive.

The importance of the distinction between progressive and frequentative force can be seen in Gen. 2:19. If a reader sees Gen. 1:1-2:3 and Gen. 2:4-25 as narratives used by an author or editor who combined them harmoniously, then each is in the context of the other. Accordingly, the fact that the first describes the creation of animals prior to the creation of mankind is occasion for giving to the consecutive imperfect at the beginning of Gen. 2:19 a frequentative force. The translation which says that God continued to form animals after he made man leaves no ground for a charge that the two narratives contradict each other at this point. This charge, which has been made often by reputable expositors of Genesis, is a result of the old method of interpreting *waw* consecutive. *Waw* consecutive was interpreted at this point as making the imperfect a consequence or an equivalent of a preceding perfect. That preceding perfect, which translators probably considered the starting point of the chain of imperfects with *waw* consecutive in 2:4-25, appears in 2:5. The concluding clause, "And *as for a man,* there was not one to till the ground," contained the negative for a substantive clause with the verb "to be" understood. That verb, if it had been written, would have been a perfect. Following it, imperfects with *waw* consecutive appear in verses 6, 7, 8, 9, 15, 16, 17, 18, 19 to tie together the narrative. Following the old interpretation of *waw* consecutive, translators have rendered the imperfect at the beginning of verse 19 as "formed," which is the translation for a perfect. The distinctive force of the imperfect is lost completely. Thus occasion has been given for the charge that the two narratives contradict each other.

The starting point of these chains may be marked in many ways. Preceding perfects frequently serve to do so. Other imperfects, participles, infinitives, and even nouns are so used. Sometimes there is no preceding word. Maybe it was not the author's desire in such cases to fix the starting point except as being somewhere in the past. The word for "and it came to pass" is the one most commonly used in this way, and it is comparable to the English phrase "once upon a time."

A graph may be made by linking the graphs of several consecutives. The upright lines, shaped as braces, will stand for the conjunctions which link the verbs to their starting points as well as the starting points themselves. (} } } } } } }).

1. In past time (Combination 10):

Gen. 5:3 — . . . then *he proceeded to beget* a son.

Since only one child is involved, the verb is a progressive imperfect. The interpretation of the verb as progressive is reflected by the auxiliary "proceeded."

Gen. 5:4 — . . . and *he continued to beget* sons and daughters.

The imperfect with *waw* consecutive is written exactly as in Gen. 5:3; the context, however, shows that the action occurred repeatedly. The auxiliary "continued" reflects the frequentative force.

The contrast observed here appears again in the following verses: Genesis 5:6 and 7; 9 and 10; 12 and 13; 15 and 16; 18 and 19; 21 and 22; 25 and 26; 28 and 30. Similar contrasts are scattered through Gen. 11:10-24.

These contrasts appear to have been introduced quite deliberately. They show, therefore, that progressive and frequentative imperfects were distinguished from perfects in all cases and also distinguished each from the other.

Gen. 12:1 — And Yahweh *continued to say* to Abram, . . .

The frequentative interpretation in this case may be seriously questioned by some. For that reason the evidence will be examined at length. This evidence does not give ground for a dogmatic opinion, but it does indicate a strong probability. This probability can be seen only by meticulous examination of the evidence.

That part of the context which provides evidence in this case includes these words from the latter part of the verse: "your country," "your kindred," and "your father's house."

"From your land" in Gen. 12:1 uses the word land separately from the word "kindred," which appears in the phrase immediately after this one. The word "land" standing alone can be applied to any land. The word "kindred" standing alone is used to describe things in general which are related to a person by that person's birth. Its most usual application is to one's kin in general. In Gen. 43:7 it is made to include brothers as well as a father. When the two words are tied together in a genitival relation, as in Gen. 11:28, each word restricts the other. The land becomes the land of one's birth or nativity, as in Haran's case. Other instances appear in Gen. 24:7; 31:13; Jer. 22:10; 46:16; Ezek. 23:15; Ruth 2:11. The kin referred to become those who gave one birth in that land — one's forefathers, one's ancestors — rather than kin in general. In Biblical usage at least the words are thus restricted when linked together.

When Abram, according to Gen. 24:4, called Charran "my land," he used "land" separately in accord with the usage described. When he, according to Gen. 24:7, referred to the land of his birth, he used "land" and kindred (forefathers) together.

Our immediate interest is in the fact that Abram had known both Ur and Charran as his land before he moved on into Canaan. Therefore, the words "from your land" could have applied to Ur at one time and to Charran at another. "From your kindred" was likewise applicable to the kindred in Ur and to the kindred in Charran. "From your father's household" also was applicable in Ur as well as in Charran.

Since all evidence observed thus far leaves the question open, it is worthwhile to take note of the fact that Jewish tradition has persistently clung to the conviction that there was a call in Ur. At least it is the oldest tradition. We ought to hesitate before we conclude there was no ground whatever for it.

Stephen, according to Acts 7:2, 3, said, "The God of glory appeared unto our father Abraham, when he was in Mesopotamia, before he dwelt in Haran, and said unto him, 'Get thee out of thy land . . . .' " (ASV). Stephen was also dogmatic. He was, however, preaching at the time he made this dogmatic statement, not writing a commentary. Probably he felt no need before his audience in Jerusalem for supporting this statement about Abraham. He seems to have taken for granted that he was voicing an established conviction about a well-known matter. Certainly he believed there was evidence to sustain his statement. He could, of course, have cited what has been presented here, but his positiveness makes it likely that he knew more than this.

These scattered and in some cases unsubstantiated bits of evidence cannot be said to be conclusive. Nevertheless, their cumulative effect is to create a probability. Accordingly, such searchers for truth as Martin Luther, John Peter Lange, Robert S. Candlish, Marcus Dods, and H. C. Leupold have been strongly inclined to accept this probability as the most probable conclusion indicated by the evidence as a whole. Lange stated his conclusion this way: "*Out of thy country* — the fatherland. The land of Mesopotamia as it embraced both Ur of the Chaldees and Haran."[2] In accord with this conclusion, A. Gosman, who translated Lange's Commentary on Chapters XII-XXXVI, added this note of his own:

> There is no improbability in the supposition that the call was repeated. And this supposition would not only reconcile the words of Stephen and Moses, but may explain the fifth verse: "And they went forth to go into the land of Canaan, and into the land of Canaan they came." Abram had left his home in obedience to the original call of God, but had not reached the land in which he was to dwell. Now, upon the second call, he not only sets forth, but continues in his migrations until he reaches Canaan, to which he was directed.[3]

In accord with the probability that exists concerning the call of Abraham, the first imperfect in Gen. 12:1 is credited with a frequentative force.

> Gen. 25:34 — Then Jacob gave to Esau bread and lentil soup, *and he proceeded to eat* and *to drink* and *to arise* and *to go his way,* and thus Esau *proceeded to despise* the birthright.

When there is only one consecutive, "and he proceeded" indicates movement and sequence in an attractive way; but when there is a chain of them, it becomes repetitious and cumbersome. If the

2. John Peter Lange, *Genesis in Commentary on the Holy Scriptures,* Philip Schaff, ed., reprint by Zondervan Publishing House (n.d.), p. 391.
3. In Lange, *op. cit.,* p. 393.

consecutives are close together, as in Gen. 25:34, this may be avoided by the use of "proceeded" in the first case, and infinitives in the others, leaving "proceeded" to be understood but not written. Otherwise synonyms of "proceed" and varied expressions conveying the idea of sequence will be needed.

Sentences, or parts of them, and even paragraphs, may intervene between the verbs in a series of consecutives. No matter how far one may be separated from others, its progress starts from some link in its own chain. Nearly always its progress starts from the link immediately preceding it, and all links form one chain. Once in a while it starts from some link further back, making two chains to start from a common source. For instance, the last verb in the example above states a logical consequence which parallels all of the preceding chain. The despising started with or before the eating and runs concurrently with the eating, the drinking, the arising, and the going.

Syntactical summary: inc-pa-ind (cons)

There are, of course, able translators who consider the translation of Hebrew imperfects in past time as perfects to be a small matter. The contrary opinion is insisted upon in what follows for the sake of those who wish to consider the matter thoroughly.

Insistence upon a distinctive meaning for any imperfect in past time is strongly supported by the use of imperfects in Arabic. Arabic is very close to Hebrew in its alphabet, vocabulary, grammar, and syntax. Its maintenance of distinctive meanings both for perfects and imperfects is, therefore, evidence that carries great weight in the interpretation of the basic ideas in these verb forms. There is probably no evidence outside the Bible itself that supports this insistence upon distinctive translations for these imperfects so strongly. This statement is not intended to say that Arabic uses imperfects everywhere that Hebrew uses them. Nevertheless, it does use them with meanings that parallel closely the Hebrew meanings which we cite. Moreover, such explanations as Arabic grammarians sometimes give in the words, "the equivalent of a perfect," are not intended to say that the two forms are the same. They do say that Arabic uses imperfects in senses equivalent to certain Latin or English perfects. A triangle and a rectangle can be equivalent, i.e., equivalent in space, yet they are not the same thing.

During the period 1941-1961, Dr. Jochanan Kapliwatsky of Jerusalem prepared a series of studies for English speaking students who are beginners in the study of Arabic. The series is entitled *Arabic Language and Grammar,* and it contains four parts with grammatical facts richly illustrated by reading exercises. Because this work is for beginners, syntactical explanations are stated as simply as possible, and repetitions involving progressive and additional explanations are scattered through the series. For that very reason they furnish very helpful guidance in consideration of this matter.

The first statement is as follows:

> The Arabic verb has two main tenses which, however, are not real tenses in their European sense. These two main tenses are generally known as Perfect and Imperfect.
>
> The Perfect denotes a finished action, most often referring to the *past,* and the Imperfect denotes an unfinished action, most often referring to the *present* or *future.*[4]

Another explanation is as follows:

> The imperfect denotes an unfinished action most often referring to the present or future. In reality, however, the time of action is expressed by an adverb, or particle.[5]

Kapliwatsky's statement amounts to the same as saying that the Arabic imperfect maintains its distinctive force at all times, and that those speaking Arabic have accommodated this verb form to ideas of tense and time by adding adverbs and particles.

Another statement is this (This is given in contrast to several dealing with the perfect and demonstrating its maintenance of a distinctive meaning in any time.):

> *Kad* followed by an Imperfect means 'sometimes' or 'perhaps,' e.g. *huwa kad yarjihu,* 'he sometimes returns' or 'perhaps he will return.'[6]

This explanation shows that, even in future time, the imperfect carries a frequentative or subjunctive force, not the singular and indicative force of the Perfect.

Yet another statement appears in this:

> To express "he used to," the perfect of *kana*[7] is used before

---

4. Jochanan Kapliwatsky, *Arabic Language and Grammar,* (Jerusalem, Palestine, Part I, Rubin Mass, 1941; fourth edition, Hamaarav Press, 1959), p. 48.

5. *Ibid.,* Part II, p. 19.

6. *Ibid.,* Part III, p. 71.

7. The pf 3rd mass sing of the verb, "to be" in Arabic.

the Imperfect of another verb, e.g. "he used to ride (out) every day three times";[8] "she used to open the door twice every day"; "and there used to be in the city a commander with a thousand men."[9]

This explanation clinches the assertion that Arabic imperfects in past time, as well as imperfects in present or future time, are used with a force as truly distinctive as those of any other verb form.

In the last sentence used to demonstrate this usage there is another feature that the student ought to take care to understand. The perfect of the verb "to be" is used before the imperfect of the same verb. The perfect emphasizes the time as past; the imperfect emphasizes the action as frequentative. This construction with the perfect and the imperfect of the same verb is quite unusual. Nevertheless, it is grammatically possible and proper. It drives home this distinctive force of the imperfect in a powerful way. The apparent parallel between this and one of the Hebrew imperfects in Ex. 3:14 is thrillingly interesting. The argument that has continued for two millenniums over the translation of that verse in the Septuagint and over the part it has played in the English translation "I am what I am" or "I am that I am" has surely confirmed the charge that "I am" is not a proper translation for a Hebrew imperfect. That translation could fit a substantive sentence with the verb "to be" understood or a characteristic perfect but not an imperfect. The first of the two imperfects of the verb "to be" in this verse could be interpreted quite fittingly as a repetition of the identical form found two verses before this one. In that case, it refers to the future. In view of the strong emphasis in the early verses of the chapter upon Yahweh's keeping of his promises to Abraham, Isaac, and Jacob, the second imperfect could be a repetition of this great truth. In such case, it is past. Translated in keeping with the example given above, the statement becomes this: "I shall continue to be what I used to be" or "I shall continue to be what I have always been." This rendering is cryptic but understandable, unusual but powerful, simple yet crowning its context with a statement of Yahweh's faithfulness so brief as to be amazing and so meaningful as to be inspiring.

8. Arabic sentences accompanying these translations have been omitted.
9. Kapliwatsky, op. cit., Part IV, p. 48.

2. In present time (Combination 11):

    Isa. 44:12 — He forges (ch pf) iron as an axe, and he works (another ch pf) with coals, and with hammers *he proceeds to fashion it,* and *thus he proceeds to work* it with the arm of his strength; also he is hungry (another ch pf) and has no strength, he drinks (another ch pf) no water; and *so he becomes faint.*

These are rare, and they follow the same pattern in translation as those in past time.

Syntactical summary: inc-pre-ind (cons)

3. In future time (Combination 12):

    Isa. 9:5; 9:6 in Eng — For a child shall be born (a pro pf) to us, a son shall be given (another pro pf) to us, and *will come to be* the rule upon his shoulder, and one *will proceed to call* his name Wonderful Counsellor, Mighty God, Everlasting Father, Prince of Peace.

These likewise are rare and constitute no new problem in translation.

Syntactical summary: inc-fut-ind (cons)

The interpretation of *waw* consecutive will be discussed further when conjunctions are dealt with. It is good to observe even now, however, that the way to a new interpretation of *waw* consecutive is opened by recognition of a distinctive character in all perfects and all imperfects. If every perfect is interpreted as having a force peculiar to perfects and every imperfect a force peculiar to imperfects, old ideas about the influence of *waw* consecutive upon them are out of place.

Consecutive imperfects are characteristic of all types of narratives. A chain of these consecutive imperfects is the thread by which all the parts of a narrative are tied together. Even as a very large portion of the Old Testament is composed mainly of narrative, so the interpretation of consecutive imperfects is a very important part of Old Testament translation and Old Testament interpretation.

Within a narrative an author may introduce other types of composition. The series of jussives in the story of creation, Gen. 1:1-2:3, is interwoven with the consecutive imperfects to define with precision the author's teaching concerning Yahweh's development of created things. A mixture of participles, incipient imperfects, and substantive clauses may be used, as in Gen. 2:10-14, for the sake of accurate and vivid description. A series of correlative perfects may be added, as in Ex. 33:8-11, to make many details of a great scene stand out in the reader's mind as actions that occurred at one and the same time. These same correlative perfects may be the author's means of presenting an extensive prophecy, as in Isa. 11:1-12:6, as a unit. When the narrative is resumed, however, a consecutive imperfect signifies the movement, the progress, the sequence of it.

To lose sight of the distinctions involved in these various types of composition leads to the loss of many clues to interpretation, at a great many places. Yet our translations have persisted in applying theories that have made the translation of consecutive imperfects and correlative perfects to be alike. For example, they have translated Gen. 1:3 this way, "And God said, Let there be light . . .," instead of saying, "And God proceeded to say, Let there be light . . .," or "Afterwards God proceeded to say, Let there be light . . . ." As a result we have been left in the dark as to what was the first act of creation affirmed by this story. Expositors have differed and disputed and left us more in the dark than ever.

English readers feel no loss as a rule, because they have been accustomed from childhood to the type of narrative used by the translators, and because they have never known any other type of composition in narrative.

Nevertheless, there is a tremendous loss!

Chapter Five

Participles

All participles are in the indicative mood. It is expedient, therefore, to consider them before turning to subjunctive imperfects and perfects in subjunctive combinations.

Participles partake of the nature of verbs and of nouns. This fact accounts for a list of peculiarities, as follows:

(1) Participles serve both as verbs and as nouns. The same form can mean "is killing" or "the one who is killing."

(2) Verbal participles are inflected like nouns. Their endings signify number and gender but not person. Therefore, their subjects must be written, there being nothing in the participle itself to indicate a pronominal subject.

(3) Verbal participles always retain the nature of a predicate complement. Evidence of this appears in the following:

a. The subject is regularly written before the participle. If a copulative verb is thought of as linking the two, as is always possible, that is the natural order. In such case the participle is a predicate complement.

b. Some form of the verb to be is occasionally put with the participle after the fashion of a periphrastic conjugation (cf. Ex. 3:1). This puts into words what is merely understood in other cases.

(4) The regular negative with a participle is *'en,* the construct state of *'ayin,* nothing. It negates the idea of being or existence, meaning is not, are not, was not, were not, etc. Obviously, then, a participle with *'en* is a noun.

(5) Passive participles serve as gerunds. Examples: *nora',* one to be feared; *nekhbadh,* one honored, or an honorable one.

All participles represent continuous states. Even in the noun there is a continuous manifestation of the state described by the verb.

This continuous state of the participle needs to be clearly distinguished from the continual state of a frequentative imperfect. A telephone line is continuous like a participle, but its poles are continual like a frequentative. Thus the graph of a participle is a long line (—————).

The difference between participles and progressive imperfects lies in their implications as to limits. Participles indicate no limitations, no point for beginning or ending, while progressives proceed from some point.

1. In past time (Combination 13):
   Gen. 18:1 — And he *was sitting* at the door of the tent.
   Gen. 37:7 — We *were binding* sheaves.
   Judg. 7:13 — And behold, there *was* a man *telling* to his comrade a dream.
Syntactical summary: cont-pa-ind

The translations suggested here are characterized by continuous aspect, as Curme describes it,[1] or by the progressive conjugation, as Opdycke describes it.[2] It is formed by adding the present participle to various forms of the verb to be when the verb is active and the past participle to progressive forms of the verb to be (i.e., I was being seen, etc.) when the verb is passive. The continuous force of the Hebrew participle is thus clearly reproduced.

English translators have been very lax in their handling of these participles. They frequently substitute for them translations which belong to other verb forms. In Gen. 18:1, AV, ASV, RSV, and MNT give us the translation of a narrative perfect, only AT handling it like a participle. In Gen. 37:7, all of them handle the participle as a participle. In Judg 7:13, all except AV do so. Why they so frequently fail to do so in other cases is hard to understand.

It is interesting to observe that in Judg. 7:13 the participle

---

1. George O. Curme, *A Grammar of the English Language* (Boston: A. C. Heath and Company, 1935), III, p. 373.
2. Opdycke, John B., *Harper's English Grammar* (New York: Harper and Brothers, 1941), p. 173.

is handled as the abridgment of a relative clause, *Who was telling to his comrade a dream.* ASV handles it this way, and this way is the exact form of the Hebrew sentence.

2. In present time (Combination 14):
  Gen. 4:10 — Your brother's blood *is crying* out to me.
  Deut. 4:1 — I *am teaching* you.
  Isa. 1:7 — Strangers *are devouring* your land.
Syntactical summary: cont-pre-ind

The present progressive clearly distinguishes these present participles from all perfects and imperfects in present time. The translations constantly use a simple present, AV and ASV doing so in Gen. 4:10; AV, ASV, RSV, and MNT in Deut. 4:1; and all of them in Isa. 1:7. What interpretation they intend to put upon their simple present is uncertain, but at least it is not distinctive. In doing so they lose much of the animation and vividness of the Hebrew. It appears possible to retain the continuous movement of the participle in all cases, and faithful efforts ought to be made to do so.

3. In future time (Combination 15):
  In future time a remarkable use is often made of the continuous idea of the participle. The progress appears to start in the present and to stretch into the future. This is a mental feat which creates a vivid and dramatic effect. It is as when one says, "I am coming," though the actual start has not yet been made, and he means, "I will indeed be coming," or "I will be coming immediately." Emphasis is thus laid on one or the other of the following thoughts: (1) The decision is being effected; and, in mind at least, progress is already under way. (2) The actual start will follow immediately.

  Occasionally, circumstances in the context show that the time is entirely future. Then we need a strictly future translation. Otherwise, we need the present-future combination to give the dramatic assurance of certainty or immediate beginning.
  Gen. 6:17 — Behold, I *am bringing* the flood, even water, upon the earth.
  Gen. 7:4 — For after seven days I *will be causing it to rain* upon the earth forty days and forty nights.

I Sam. 19:11 — If you are not delivering your life tonight, tomorrow, you will be a dead man (lit. one made to die).

II Sam. 12:23 — I *am going* to him, but he cannot return to me.

II Sam. 20:21 — And the woman said to Joab, Behold, his head *is being thrown* to you over the wall.

Syntactical summary: cont-fut or pre + fut-ind

Again the progressive conjugation appears to be the only expression capable of carrying the force of the participle. MNT uses it in Gen. 6:17 and II Sam. 12:23. AT uses several interesting paraphrases for it, seemingly intended to express the present-future force described above. These are "am about to bring" in Gen. 6:17, "am going to make it rain" in Gen. 7:4, and "expect to go" in II Sam. 12:23. Something of this sort is doubtless good in Gen. 7:4, where we have a pure future, but elsewhere they seem weak. "I am about to come" is a weak expression as compared with "I am coming," when someone is waiting for you. Translations with "about" in them cannot adequately represent participles in present-future time. The woman talking to Joab in II Sam. 20:21 and saying, "His head is being thrown to you over the wall," was not making a promise about the future time but giving a vivid picture of immediate action. Likewise, David speaking of his dead child in II Sam. 12:23 was not putting off his progress toward a reunion into the indefinite future but saying, as it were, "From this moment I am on my way to join him."

Chapter Six

Subjunctives

Whereas *indicatives* represent ideas as *realities* (cf. p. 32), *subjunctives* represent them as *mental conceptions,* ideas apprehended by reason or imagination only. In Hebrew three main types of subjunctives appear: (1) contrary-to-fact, (2) potential, (3) optative. The contrary-to-fact type combines perfects and participles with certain particles to show that the unreality of an idea is fixed and permanent, i.e., it is impossible. The potential uses the imperfect to indicate that something is possible. The optative uses the imperfect, usually with additions or changes to mark its special force, to show that something is not merely possible but also desired by the author.

I

CONTRARY-TO-FACT SUBJUNCTIVES

Occasionally a perfect or a participle is brought into a combination which associates it with a subjunctive idea. This at first seems very strange, and we must observe closely the particles with which it is combined to understand the effect. The verb itself is never actually subjunctive, for it retains the full force of its certainty; the combination, however, indicates a contrary-to-fact idea and is thus subjunctive. This is true in contrary-to-fact conditional sentences and in rhetorical questions.

1. Conditions with *lu* or *lule* (Combination 16):
   Judg. 8:19 — *If* you *had kept* them *alive, I would not have slain* you.

74

Isa. 1:9 — *Except* Yahweh of hosts *had left* us a very small remnant, as Sodom had we been.

Ps. 81:14-15; 81:13-14 in Eng — *If* my *people* were *listening* to me . . . I *would soon subdue* their enemies.

Syntactical summary: com-pre-con subj

In these contrary-to-fact conditional sentences a special introductory particle, either *lu* or *lule,* is used to indicate that the condition is contrary-to-fact. After it a perfect may be used both in the protasis and apodosis. The perfect in the protasis appears to indicate that the condition stated in such a clause is non-existent and impossible. The perfect in the apodosis appears to indicate that the conclusion based upon the contrary-to-fact condition is as fixed in impossibility as the condition itself. The effect of the particle upon each of these verbs, though the particle appears only before the first, conveys ideas called by us subjunctive. This is true because we call all imaginary or contrary-to-fact ideas subjunctive. Nevertheless, these perfects are still single, finished, and certain; and they should not be identified with the Hebrew subjunctive imperfects which are subjunctive by reason of their own nature. It is the combination, not the perfect alone, that approximates our English subjunctive. This forcing of contingency and certainty into the same statement is very rarely done, but it furnishes a peculiarly dramatic expression which creates an impression of unavoidable obligation or inescapable necessity.

Only in Num. 22:33 does any other particle than *lu* or *lule* appear with a perfect in these conditions. Moreover, the appearance there of *'ulay,* perhaps, does not make sense. So the following bit of advice appears to be correct: "Read *lu* for *'ulay* in Numbers 22:33."[1] These facts make it easy to detect the use of such conditions by the presence of *lu* or *lule.*

When imperfects appear in these contrary-to-fact conditional sentences, nothing strange or peculiar is involved. *Lu* or *lule* provides a context that signifies the subjunctive mood.

2. Rhetorical questions (Combination 17):

Num. 23:10 — *Who can count* the dust of Jacob?

Isa. 53:1 — *Who can believe* our report; and, as for the arm of Yahweh, upon whom *can it be revealed?*

---

1. Brown, Driver, and Briggs, *A Hebrew and English Lexicon of the Old Testament* (New York: Houghton Mifflin Co., 1906), p. 530.

Jer. 30:21 — For *who* is there that *could be security* for his own heart in order to come near to me?

Syntactical summary: com-fut-con subj

These questions are distinguished by the fact that they apply to future time and use a perfect with *mi,* who?.   An imperfect with *mi* in future time would ask an ordinary, open question like this: "Who will go for us?" (Isa. 6:8).   A perfect with *mi* in past time would also ask an open question like this: "Who told you that you were naked?" (Gen. 3:11).   In the rhetorical question, the perfect nullifies the normal implications of the interrogative, showing that it is not truly an interrogative but is put there merely for rhetorical effect; and the interrogative nullifies the normal implications of the perfect, showing that it is not a mark of reality but is put there to establish the certainty of a negative answer.

The perfect with *mi* in Gen. 21:7 has generally been interpreted as subjunctive.   Because the reference is apparently to the past, the following interpretation is preferred:

Gen. 21:7 — And she went on to say, *Who spoke* a word to Abraham, (saying), Sarah shall suckle children?   Yet indeed I have borne him a son in his old age.

II

POTENTIAL SUBJUNCTIVES

The partially assured, tentative aspect of the imperfect is utilized in a potential subjunctive.   *lu* may be added in some cases, but as a rule only the context is relied upon to mark it as subjunctive rather than indicative.   Those evidences out of the context which mark its state as possible rather than real may be classified as follows: (1) those indicating or questioning the mere possibility of it;   (2) those indicating or questioning desire concerning it; (3) those indicating or questioning responsibility for doing it.   Any such indication or question reflects the fact that a thing does not already exist but is merely possible.

1. Subjunctives of mere possibility (Combination 18):
    Gen. 13:16 — If a man *could be able* to number the dust of the earth, also your seed *could be numbered.*
    Deut. 1:12 — How *can I bear* alone your cumbrance?
    Isa. 1:18 — Though your sins *be* as scarlet, they *may be* made white as snow.

Psa. 24:3 — Who *may ascend* into the hill of Yahweh?

Syntactical summary: inc-fut-pot subj (pos)

2. Subjunctives of desire (Combination 18):

I Kings 13:8 — If you *would give* me half your house, I could not go in with you.

The subjunctives of desire are distinguished from the optative subjunctives by the fact that desire in the potentials arises from some other source than the author while desire in optatives does arise from the author.

Ruth 1:13 — *Would* you therefore *tarry* till they were grown?

Syntactical summary: inc-fut-pot subj (des)

3. Subjunctives of responsibility (Combination 18):

Ex. 3:11 — Who am I that I *should go* to Pharaoh?

I Chron. 12:33, 12:32 in Eng — To know what Israel *ought to do.*

Syntactical summary: inc-fut-pot subj (res)

All of these subjunctive imperfects are in future time, and this fact helps to mark them.

Translation needs to vary only so much as is necessary to express the ideas of mere possibility, desire, or responsibility.

III

OPTATIVE SUBJUNCTIVES

Two modified forms of the imperfect are used to express an author's desire, urge, or feeling. The first person is used to express an exhortation or cohortation affecting the speaker or a group of which he is a part; so this form is called cohortative. The second or third person is used to enjoin another or others; so these forms are called jussives.

External marks are generally used to identify these two forms beyond question. On the other hand, it is evident from many texts that an imperfect without any mark other than its relation to the context may bear the optative force, especially as a jussive. In rare instances (cf. Deut. 33:16; Isa. 5:19; and Ps. 20:4) the sign of the cohortative appears on a jussive. On the other hand, the internal vowel change customary with the jussive appears in some of those cohortatives to which cohortative *h* could not be added. These facts seem to indicate that these two forms of the optative subjunctive were considered so much alike in nature that the usual mark of either could be used with the other if there was likelihood of its not being recognized for lack of an external mark. In any case the extensive efforts made to mark these two forms lays upon us an obligation to respect their peculiar force wherever it can be discerned and likewise to avoid construing an imperfect without marks as an optative unless the evidence from the context appears to be decisive.

1. Cohortatives:

Cohortatives express the author's desire, urge, or feeling concerning himself and do so by direct reference to himself, using pronouns in the first person. When the speaker refers to himself alone, the cohortative may express determination, request, or willingness; when he is free, determination; when he is entreating another for permission, request; when he is yielding agreeably to inevitable consequences, willingness. If the speaker includes others, the cohortative expresses exhortation.

(1) Determination (Combination 19):

Deut. 17:14 — *I will set* a king over me. (Or) *I am determined to set* a king over me.

Gen. 17:2 — And *I will make* my covenant between me and you that I may increase you exceedingly. (Or) For *I am determined* to make (set or establish) my covenant between me and you that I may increase you exceedingly.

Ex. 3:3 — *I will turn aside* now that I may see this great sight. (Or) *I am determined to turn aside* now that I may see this great sight.

Hos. 13:14 — *I will be* your plagues, O death; *I will be* your destruction, O Sheol. (Or) *I am determined to be* your plagues, O death; *I am determined to be* your destruction, O Sheol.

Syntactical summary: inc-fut-opt subj (coh of det)

If the auxiliary "will" is used with cohortatives, we have the problem of distinguishing them from perfects of confidence in the first person. The problem can be solved in either of two ways: (1) using emphatic auxiliaries with perfects of confidence and will with cohortatives; (2) using "will" with perfects of confidence in first person and using "determined," "intend," and the like with infinitives to express the force of cohortatives. Perhaps the latter is best.

Because translators have often interpreted as cohortatives verbs not marked as such in the Hebrew and, on the other hand, have failed to interpret as cohortatives some that are marked as such in Hebrew, we need to note with care the marks that are used. In the foregoing a cohortative *h* is added to the verb in Deut. 17:14; Gen. 17:2; Ex. 3:3; while in Hos. 13:14 there is a shift of accent and consequent vowel change. This shift of accent and vowel change are the same changes that occur frequently in jussives. Both in cohortatives and jussives these changes are due to an added stress in pronunciation, which is produced by the urgency of the mood and pulls the accent backward. They are rare in cohortatives, and this is probably due to the fact that the cohortative *h* can be added in the great majority of them. In Hos. 13:14 *h* could not be added because the verb itself ended in *h*. As seen in Judg. 18:4, the same change with the same verb is produced by *waw* consecutive, for it also draws the accent backward; but the two forms found here, without any conjunction, can be explained only as cohortatives or errors.

In this same connection it is exceedingly interesting to observe in Gen. 17:2 and Ex. 3:3 that the second verb is a *l-h* verb in both cases, attached to a simple *waw,* and without a shift of accent or a vowel change. The absence of all external marks leads to the conclusion that these are not cohortatives, as all the translations have made them, but parts of subordinate, subjunctive clauses. (Cf. Purpose and Result Clauses, the treatment of which comes later.)

On the other hand, the obvious marks of an optative in both verbs cited in Hos. 13:14, plus the fact that a cohortative interpretation fits the context, lead to the conclusion that those are cohortatives. Only AV and a note in ASV and RSV recognized them. Nevertheless the evidence appears incontestable. Moreover, neglect of them, and the neglect of many other optatives, appears to be one of the very serious failures of our translations.

The fitness of these two cohortatives is strongly indicated by all parts of the chapter in which they appear. Verse 14 makes this quite obvious when translated thus:

> From the power of Sheol, I shall ransom them;
> from death, I shall redeem them;
> *I am determined to be* your plagues, O death;
> I am determined to be your destruction, O Sheol;
> any change of mind will be hidden from mine eyes.

The importance of this interpretation is seen when we observe this word as a messianic prophecy and link it with two preceding ones in Hosea and with those that follow in Isaiah. Hos. 3:5 identifies the Yahweh who promises to save Israel, despite all her terrible sins, with David their king (the Second David). Hos. 11:9 calls this Saviour "The Holy One in the midst of thee," the transcendent one who makes himself immanent in Israel. Hosea's description prepares the way for Isaiah's marvelous use of "the Holy One of Israel" as a means of tying together all his pictures of Messiah as the God-man. This same verse stresses the assurance that the Holy One will not come in wrath. Thus it prepares the way for the assurance of Hos. 13:14 and for the incomparable picture of the Messiah who dies in Israel's stead given in Isa. 52:13-53:12. What a tragedy it is to have one of the links in this golden chain lost by unfaithful translations!

(2) Request (Combination 19):
Gen. 50:5 — *Let me go up,* I pray.
Ex. 3:18 — And now *let us go,* we pray.
Deut. 2:27 — *Let me pass through* your land.
Ps. 25:2 — *Let me* not *be ashamed.*

Syntactical summary: inc-fut-opt subj (coh of req)

The negative *'al* (cf. Ps. 25:2) is another of the special marks of an optative. The particle of entreaty (I pray! or, please!) is in accord with the urge of an optative; but it also appears frequently with imperatives, and it is not a characteristic of either.

(3) Willingness (Combination 19):
Gen. 46:30 — *I am willing to die* at this time.
Isa. 38:10 — *I am willing to go* into the gates of Sheol.
Ps. 4:9; 4:8 in Eng — In peace *I am ready both to lie down and to sleep.*

Syntactical summary: inc-fut-opt subj (coh of will)

The "let me die" of AV, ASV, RSV, and MNT, in Gen. 46:30, — AT does not recognize the cohortative — does not appear to be the best translation. It is the language of request, and a request should be addressed to the one exercising control over it. The apparent intent of the cohortative in this case is to express mere willingness.

In Isa. 38:10 both MNT and AT seek to give a special force to the cohortative, but they make it a potential rather than an optative subjunctive. The interpretation given by BDB to the preceding phrase, in connection with the *domi* (cessation), helps to clarify the fitness of the interpretation given here.[2]

In Ps. 4:8, AV, ASV, RSV, and AT recognize the jussive but seem to interpret it as expressing determination. Perhaps David did not feel at the time that rest and sleep were under his control.

(4) Exhortation (Combination 19):

Ps. 2:3 — *Let us break asunder* their bands and *let us cast away* their cords from us.

Gen. 24:57 — And *let us inquire* at her mouth.

Isa. 1:18 — Come now and *let us prove* each other.

Jonah 1:7 — And *let us cast lots*.

Syntactical summary: inc-fut-opt subj (coh of exh)

2. Jussives:

Jussives express the author's desire, urge, or feeling concerning other things than himself. The author may use a jussive to express a wish that actually applies to himself; but, in doing so, he uses the third person as though speaking of another, and only the context reveals the fact that he is thinking of himself.

When the jussive refers to persons or matters over which the author exercises authority, it may express a polite command, a decree, or a permission. Otherwise, it may express a petition, a suggestion, a wish, or mere acquiescence.

(1) Polite command (Combination 20):

Prov. 3:7 — *Do* not *be wise* in your own eyes.

Deut. 15:3 — *Let* your hand *release* it.

I Kings 20:8 — *Do* not *listen*.

Syntactical summary: inc-fut-opt subj (jus of com)

In these instances the author expresses his will concerning the person to whom he is speaking and over whom he assumes control.

Signs appear as follows: in Prov. 3:7, the negative and a shift of accent followed by apocopation; in Deut. 15:3, a vowel change; and in I Kings 20:8, the negative *'al*.

(2) Permission (Combination 20):

Ezra 1:3 — *Let him go up* and *let him build*.

I Kings 13:33 — Whoever was willing (lit, the willing one), to him he proceeded to give authority, (saying), Yea, *let him be* among the priests of the high places.

Isa. 45:21 — Yea, *let them take counsel* together.

2. *Ibid.*, p. 198.

Syntactical summary: inc-fut-opt subj (jus of per)

In these instances the author expresses his will concerning a person or persons to whom he is not speaking, but over whom he assumes control.

The signs appear as follows: in Ezra 1:3 and I Kings 13:33, a shift of accent and vowel change; in Isa. 45:21 the context alone is depended upon, the command to declare which opens the verse making an indicative out of place and an optative the expression that fits.

In I Kings 13:33 we have one of many instances in which grammarians claim that there is a copyist's error[3] or else the jussive has lost its force and should be handled as an ordinary perfect.[4] Driver claims that this construction is in past time and therefore turns it into a purpose clause.[5] All of these arguments are obviated by understanding that we have here a quotation of the permission Jeroboam issued to anyone willing to serve in his new priesthood. As a quotation the time becomes future. As a quotation the jussive fits, for it is synonymous with the preceding statement, "he proceeded to give authority" (lit, he proceeded to fill his hand; or, he proceeded to make full his power.) Omission of the word "saying" was not strange in Hebrew. Isa. 45:14 furnishes another instance of its omission before a quotation. Moreover, a jussive or cohortative with a *waw* conjunctive that relates it to a person other than its subject seems to have been understood as evidence of a quotation. Hos. 11:4 furnishes a good example: With cords of a man I proceeded to draw them, with bands of love; and so I became to them as one lifting a yoke off their jaws (saying), Yea, I will set food before them.

    (3) Decree (Combination 20):

        Gen. 1:3 — *Let* there *be* light.

        Gen. 1:9 — *Let* the waters *be collected* . . . and *let* the dry
        land *be seen.*

        Esther 7:2 — What is your request, Queen Esther? Yea,
        let it be granted you.

---

3. E. Kautzsch, *Gesenius' Hebrew Grammar,* 28th ed. (Oxford: The Clarendon Press, 1910), p. 322f.

4. *Ibid.,* p. 323.

5. S. R. Driver, *A Treatise on the Use of the Tenses in Hebrew,* (3rd ed., Oxford: The Clarendon Press, 1892). p. 67, sec. 63.

Syntactical summary: inc-fut-opt subj (jus of dec)

In these instances the author expresses his will concerning an event or condition over which he assumes control but without speaking to a particular person. In Esther 7:2, the king is speaking in Esther's presence and for her benefit, but he is not addressing his decree to her.

In Gen. 1:9, the context alone indicates a jussive, the organization of the story of creation being such as to indicate that the verb is part of a series of divine decrees, beginning in 1:3 and 1:6 with forms that are unmistakably jussives. In Esther 7:2, the apocopation of the *l-h* verb marks the jussive, though the fact that it is in pause has prevented its accent from shifting.

> (4) Petition (Combination 20):
>
> Gen. 44:33 — *Let* your servant *remain,* I pray.
>
> I Kings 8:26 — And now, O God of Israel, *let* your word *be fulfilled,* I pray.
>
> Gen. 19:20 — And *let* my soul *live.*
>
> Gen. 18:30 — O *let* not the Lord *be angry.*

Syntactical summary: inc-fut-opt subj (jus of pet)

In these instances the author is expressing his will concerning himself to another person who has control over him. He does so by the indirect method of referring to himself in the third person.

The usual signs appear in all cases. In I Kings 8:26, the ultima has a *metheg* to insure pronunciation of its vowel, but the *mehuppakh* on the penult marks the main accent and the shift that has taken place.

> (5) Suggestion (Combination 20):
>
> Gen. 41:33 — *Let* Pharaoh *look out* a man.
>
> I Kings 1:2 — *Let* there *be sought* . . . a young woman.
>
> I Kings 22:8 — *Let* not the king *say* so.

Syntactical summary: inc-fut-opt subj (jus of sug)

In these instances the author is expressing his will concerning another person over whom he does not assume control.

In I Kings 1:2 only the context marks the jussive. It introduces a proposition which cannot be a command because it is spoken by servants to their king. It is shown by the preceding verse to be an expression of will concerning another person over whom these servants do not have control.

> (6) Wish (Combination 20):
>
> I Sam. 1:23 — Only *let* Yahweh *establish* his word.

Ps. 14:7 — O that the salvation of Israel *would come out* of Zion.

Gen. 30:34 — Behold! Would that (it were so)! *Let it be* according to your word.

Syntactical summary: inc-fut-opt subj (jus of wish)

In these instances the author expresses his will concerning events or conditions over which he does not assume control but whose fulfillment he does desire.

In each of these cases the jussive is either part of or preceded by an exclamation that helps to mark it. In I Sam. 1:23 it is *'akh,* only!; in Ps. 14:7, it is the idiomatic expression *mi yitten,* Who will give? — Would that!; in Gen. 30:34, *lu,* Would that! Translations have made this *lu* of Gen. 30:34 a part of the expression that follows it, but the massoretic text handles it as an exclamation, separate from the jussive that follows.

(7) Acquiescence (Combination 20):

Gen. 49:17 — *Let* Dan *be* a serpent by the way.

Mic. 1:2 — *Let* the Lord Yahweh *be* a witness against you.

Eccles. 12:6 — (Saying) Yea, *let* the pitcher *be broken* at the fountain.

Isa. 6:9 — Hear, keeping on hearing, but *do not perceive.*

An author uses a jussive at times to express his state of mind concerning events or conditions which he neither controls nor wishes but does accept as inevitable because they are the will of God. The jussive alone deals with the immediate situation. The context may indicate a hope of change later, as in Gen. 49:17, 18, or the lack of such hope, as in Isa. 6:9, 10, but the jussive alone does not reflect anything concerning the author's thought about a change. It expresses mere acquiescence in, submission to, or resignation to the will of God. This type of jussive, therefore, may be called quite appropriately a jussive of acquiescence.

In Eccles. 12:6, all translations have reduced the jussive to the level of a long line of imperfects preceding it which are not marked as jussives. In doing so they lose the climactic stroke of a surpassingly beautiful word picture, in which the aged one resigns himself to the inevitable approach of death.

In Mic. 1:2 all translations except MNT have recognized the jussive in an acceptable way. When Moffatt translates this way,

"The Eternal has a warning for you," he merely paraphrases. The fact that he resorted to paraphrase reflects his recognition of a problem. Instead of solving it, he alters the text.

We need to realize that this jussive is in the third person. It is not, therefore, a mere continuation of the imperatives used just before and thus a plea to the people that they permit Yahweh to bear his witness. They were commanded immediately before to listen to it, for it was a matter of deepest concern to them. This jussive, however, adds something different from a command. It is recognition of a moral necessity that Yahweh's witness against Samaria and Jerusalem be heard among the peoples of the earth as a justification of the terrible punishment to be brought upon them. This witness is a witness which condemns his people, shuts them up to judgment, and leaves them subject to the punishment of captivity. Certainly the prophet did not request or suggest or wish for this terrible punishment of his people. He did, however, express his acquiescence in it, realizing that the sin of his people on the one hand and the justice of God on the other required it. Accordingly, the prophet uses cohortatives of willingness in verses 8, 9 below, crying out, "I am ready to lament and wail, I am ready to go stripped and naked, . . . for her wounds are incurable. . . ."

Gen. 49:17 is part of a statement that includes Gen. 49:18, as follows:

Let Dan *continue as a snake* in the grass. . . . For thy salvation
do I wait, O Yahweh.

In this case AV, ASV, RSV have handled the jussive of verse 17 like a prophetic perfect. MNT has handled it like a characteristic perfect. AT does recognize the presence of a jussive but handles it like a wish. None of these is accurate, for Jacob does not wish Dan to be like a snake, nor does he expect him to continue so forever. Recognizing that he is so at the time, he acquiesces in the expectation of his continuing that way until God works a change. His anticipation of that change is revealed by the verse that follows, "*For thy salvation* do I wait, O Yahweh."

Isa. 6:9 is part of a command that includes Isa. 6:10, as follows:

Then he said, "Go, and you shall say to this people, 'Hear, keeping on hearing, but *do not perceive* [the meaning]; yea see, keeping on seeing, but *do not understand* [the message].' " Cause the heart of this people to be fat, and their ears heavy, and their eyes shut, That it may not be possible for their eyes to see, and for their ears to hear, and for their heart to understand, and that they shall repent, and that there shall be healing for them.

In this case, two special points of syntax are involved. The first applies to the adverbial phrases following the imperatives in verse 9, and the second applies to the jussives themselves indicated by the "do not" of the translation.

The adverbial phrases, "keeping on hearing" and "keeping on seeing," represent infinitives absolute that follow the imperatives, "hear" and "see." If they had preceded, they would have signified certainty, but in that they follow they signify continuance. AV and ASV first rendered them as expressing certainty but added notes afterwards to signify continuance. DV, MNT, AT, and RSV have used various expressions but definitely agree in signifying continuance. This is important for the reason that continuance of hearing without understanding at any point is that which dulls the spiritual senses to the point of finally killing those senses. In other words, these adverbs of continuance describe the experience of the people that would result in spiritual insensibility, and the jussives describe acquiescence on the part of the prophet in that inevitable fact.

The jussives have been ignored, or at least obscured, by all of these translations except RSV. They make these jussives to appear exactly like imperatives. The point of acquiescence, with its deep sense of regret accompanied by unequivocal resignation, is lacking. These failures are doubtless due to recognition of a very difficult problem that appears here without adequate appreciation of the solution.

At first glance the jussives signified by the negative "do not" seem to involve an enigma which defies understanding. The command to hear and the command to see appear to be mockery in view of the urge not to perceive the meaning and the urge not to understand the message. Since the message of a prophet was supposed to be delivered in sincerity, thus a command to hear to be accompanied by a desire that those hearing should hear with understanding, the explanation that follows it to the effect that hearing would be impossible presents quite a puzzle.

First of all, the distinction made between the message the prophet was to deliver and the effect of that message needs to be carefully observed. The two commands in verse 9, "hear" and "see," followed by the two jussives, "do not perceive" and "do not understand," are the message. The description of its effect begins with the word "cause" in verse 10 and includes everything which follows. This distinction is recognized in AT and RSV.

The two jussives were intended to signify the prophet's realization of the people's failure to receive or understand his message. This would be contrary to a prophet's normal hope, but it would also be a correct observation of the results. He would be forced to acquiesce in this fact. Evidently, Yahweh taught his prophet to use these jussives in order to prepare him to expect this denial of his normal hope and to steel his heart against the bitterness of disappointment. He could know at least that he had been obedient and that he had done his best.

The Lord's command in verse 10 that his prophet should cause ears to be heavy, eyes to be shut, and so on, was a command to keep on prophesying even though the prophesying would produce this effect in hearts that would not heed. Because the people would not receive the message, their hearts would be hardened by it. Their refusal to heed would result in complete loss of spiritual sensitivity or capacity for understanding. Thus the very same message that would bring salvation to believers would bring spiritual blindness and damnation to those who would harden their hearts against it. According to this last verse there was no hope for a change in the masses of the people of Isaiah's day. The difference between them and Dan was that a fixed state of mind and heart, a loss of the capacity for spiritual perception, would ultimately be involved in their case, while only habits of life were involved in Dan's case. As long as spiritual perception is possible, a change of mind and heart is possible; thus a change of life and destiny is possible.

Syntactical summary: inc-fut-opt subj (jus of acq)

Chapter Seven

Imperatives

In dealing with imperatives it needs to be remembered that they have the same ground form as the imperfect. This signifies that the two are closely similar in nature, and it helps to explain the fact that both the imperfect and the special form of the imperative are used as imperatives. Furthermore, we observe the following: (1) imperative imperfects are used both in positive and negative commands; (2) the special imperative form is used in positive commands only; (3) the *h* which is added regularly to cohortative imperfects is occasionally added to the special form of the imperative. This gives us three types of imperatives to consider.

It has been customary to disregard the question of state in connection with all imperatives. This is natural in view of the fact that mood is so prominent. Nevertheless, there is a contemplated state in connection with any imperative as surely as there is with any potential subjunctive, cohortative, or jussive. In all these cases the state is a mental conception, but in this subjective sense their states do exist.

I

IMPERATIVE IMPERFECTS
(Combination 21)

Gen. 3:14 — Upon your belly *you shall go* and dust *you shall eat.*

Ex. 7:2 — As for you, *you shall speak* all that I command you.

Josh. 8:7 — Then, as for you, *you shall arise* from the ambush.

Ex. 20:9 — Six days *shall you labor.*

Gen. 2:17 — But from the tree of the knowledge of good and evil *you shall* not *eat.*

Ex. 20:3 — *You shall* not *have* other gods before me.

Ex. 20:15 — *You shall* not *steal.*

Syntactical summary: inc-fut-imv (imp)

The emphases, which seem to accompany all imperative imperfects, may be the key to choices between imperative imperfects and special forms of the imperative. The imperfects place preformatives for person, number, and gender ahead of the verbal idea and then permit emphatic words, including the negative, to be used ahead of the preformatives. It is also true that they are always used for negative imperatives. The special forms of the imperative, on the other hand, put the verbal idea first and never associate with a negative. These facts point toward two conclusions: (1) Negative imperatives always use the imperfect because it is the only one that permits emphasis upon the negative. (2) Positive imperatives use the imperfect when there is an emphasis upon something other than the verbal idea, and the special form when the emphasis is to be upon the verbal idea itself.

The following distinctions between prohibitions expressed by the imperfect and prohibitions expressed by the jussive are very helpful. "In prohibition, (1) in the second person, the ordinary imperfect takes *lo'* and means *thou shalt not,* the jussive takes *'al* and means *do not;* (2) in the third person, the ordinary imperfect takes *lo'* and means *he shall not,* the jussive takes *'al* and means *let him not.*"[1]

There is very little conflict in the use of "shall" between imperative imperfects and prophetic perfects because imperative imperfects are necessarily in the second person and prophetic perfects nearly always in the third person.

II

IMPERATIVES USING THE SPECIAL FORM
(Combination 22)

Ex. 6:11 — *Go in, speak* to Pharaoh.

Ex. 4:7 — *Return* your hand into your bosom.

1. W. R. Harper, *Elements of Hebrew Syntax* (New York: Charles Scribner's Sons, 1888), p. 67.

Ex. 20:12 — *Honour* your father and your mother.
Syntactical summary: inc-fut-imv

In order to retain clearly the distinctions between the special forms and the imperfects, translators should keep the verbal idea first. Whereas the imperative imperfect of "kill" says, "You shall kill," the special imperative says, "Kill."

III

IMPERATIVES WITH *h* ADDED
(Combination 23)

Ex. 3:10 — *Come now — please!* — that I may send you.
Ps. 44:27; 44:26 in Eng — *Arise, O do arise!* To our help!
Ps. 51:14; 51:12 in Eng — *Restore* unto me — *I beg of thee* —
    the joy of my salvation.
Syntactical summary: inc-fut-imv + jus

The addition of the jussive idea emphasizes the earnestness of the command, indicating that the author not merely commands but also urgently pleads for compliance. To render these forms as mere imperatives, as our translations usually do, is to ignore some of the heart throbs of the Bible.

Since imperatives are always in the second person, it is obvious that the *h* is used with them to indicate a jussive force. This is another evidence that the cohortative and jussive are so identified that their external marks can be switched from one to the other.

Chapter Eight

Infinitives

Infinitives are verb forms but not verbs. Essentially they are nominal in their nature, naming the state of the verb. At the same time they retain certain verbal characteristics.

Infinitives manifest the character of a noun in the following ways: (1) they serve as subjects; (2) they serve as objects; (3) they are put in construct relations (genitive relations) with other nouns.

Infinitives retain verbal characteristics but never serve as verbs. Like a verb they may have an object when they stand in phrases or clauses. At times they are used where we expect imperatives or other forms. Grammarians have reasoned that they are the equivalent of various other forms.[1] However, there appears to be no sufficient reason for doing so. (Cf. Ex. 20:8; II Kings 5:10; Isa. 7:11 below.)

Infinitives absolute and infinitives construct are distinguished in meaning as well as form. The infinitives absolute name the state of the verb in an absolute or unrelated sense; so they cannot be tied into the sentence by prepositions, possessive pronouns, or the construct relation. The infinitives construct, on the other hand, do relate themselves to the sentence by means of prepositions, possessive pronouns, and construct relation.

I

INFINITIVES ABSOLUTE

Infinitives absolute may serve as nouns (gerunds), adverbs, or governing words in adverbial phrases.

1. E. Kautzsch, *Gesenius' Hebrew Grammar*, (28th ed., Oxford: The Charendon Press, 1910), p. 345.

1. Gerunds:
    (1) Serving as subjects:
        II Kings 4:43 — *Eating* and *leaving* over [will there be].
        I Kings 22:30 — *Disguising* and *coming* into the battle
           [will it be for me]; but, as for you, put on your [kingly]
           garments.
        II Kings 5:10 — *Going on* [shall there be], and you shall
           wash seven times in the Jordan.

Syntactical summary: inf abs as sub

(Descriptions of state, time, and mood are omitted, because we no longer deal with verbs.)

As a noun, the infinitive absolute is a strong, independent, striking expression used for dramatic effect. No matter whether it serves as a subject or as an object, this is true. As a subject, it often has no written verb, the verb "to be" being understood, of course, but the word standing dramatically alone.

Such paraphrases as are used by our translations do not do much harm in these cases. However, they do obscure the fact that an infinitive absolute is used, and the habit of changing the form of expression chosen by the author leads to serious loss in other places. In II Kings 5:10, we easily conclude that the infinitive has the force of an imperative. Still, it is true that the infinitive puts emphasis upon the fact that going on is a necessity rather than upon the idea that the prophet is merely commanding Naaman to go on.

    (2) Serving as objects:
        Jer. 23:14 — I see *committing adultery* and *walking* in lies.
        Isa. 22:13 — Behold *slaying* oxen and *killing* sheep, *eating* flesh and *drinking* wine;
        Isa. 1:16, 17 — Cease *doing* evil; learn *doing* good.

Syntactical summary: inf abs as obj

The power of the infinitive to control an object of its own, even while the two together serve as the object of the verb, appears clearly here. This power is a retention of verbal nature.

2. Adverbs:

As an adverb, the infinitive absolute sometimes comes into common use with any verb, but generally it is reserved for use with perfects and imperfects from its own root. In the latter sense it may emphasize the intensity or the certainty, the continuance or the completeness of the verbal action it modifies. When emphasizing intensity or certainty, it regularly precedes its verb. When emphasizing continuance or completeness, it follows its verb. Sometimes it is accompanied by *halokh,* going on, or a similar form, to magnify continuance yet more.

(1) Common adverbs:

Deut. 9:21 — I took the calf . . . and stamped it, *grinding thoroughly.*

Mic. 6:8 — And walking *humbly* with your God.

Neh. 2:2 — And so I became *very much* afraid.

Syntactical summary: inf abs as adv

(2) Emphatic adverbs signifying intensity or certainty:

Gen. 2:17 — You will *surely* die (lit, *dying,* you will die).

Ex. 21:28 — The ox should *certainly* be stoned.

I Sam. 20:6 — It was *urgently* requested of me.

Syntactical summary: inf abs as adv (cer or int)

(3) Adverbs signifying continuance or completeness:

Gen. 8:7 — And it proceeded to go forth, *continually* going to and fro.

II Sam. 3:16 — And he went on, *weeping more and more.*

II Sam. 3:24 — And he proceeded to go, *going completely away.*

Gen. 26:13 — And the man became great and continued to go forward, *becoming greater and greater.*

Syntactical summary: inf abs as adv (cont or com)

3. Governing Words in Adverbial Phrases:

Gen. 12:9 — And Abram journeyed, *going on* and *traveling* toward the south.

Ex. 20:8, 9 — *Remembering* the sabbath day in order to keep it holy, six days you shall labor.

Isa. 7:11 — Ask for yourself a sign from Yahweh your God, *making* it deep to Sheol or *making* it high to heaven.

Syntactical summary: inf abs in adv phr

In Ex. 20:8, 9 we see the damage done by turning the infinitive absolute into an imperative. As an imperative it makes verse 8 to stand alone. When all of verse 8 is seen as an adverbial phrase, it cannot stand alone. It modifies the verb of verse 9, "you shall labor," and explains the emphasis upon the "six days" of that service. In other words, the two verbs together command us to work six days with a view to consecration of the seventh to rest and worship.

In Isa. 7:11, the first form may be either imperative or infinitive absolute, while the second is definitely an infinitive absolute. Because the first is parallel to the second, each citing an extreme in a context calling for extremes, exegesis seems to require that it be interpreted as an infinitive absolute. As such it must govern the word following. That word by itself could be interpreted as "ask it — please!" or "to Sheol." As an imperative that word is repetitious at a moment calling for utmost brevity and force; and it destroys the striking description of extremes, which were evidently intended to furnish climatic force to the prophet's statement. With the infinitive absolute as a governing word, "to Sheol" is the only meaning that fits the second word. Thus interpreted the power of the prophet's words is tremendous.

II

INFINITIVES CONSTRUCT

Infinitives construct serve only as nouns. They may be subjects of verbs, objects of verbs, genitives of other nouns, or objects of prepositions.

1. Subjects of verbs:
   Gen. 2:18 — Man's *being* alone is not good.
   I Sam. 18:23 — Is it a small thing *to make one's self* a son-in-law to a king?
   Isa. 7:13 — Is the *wearying* of men a small thing to you?
   Syntactical summary: inf con as sub

2. Objects of verbs:
   I Kings 3:7 — I know not *to go out* or *to come in.*
   Num. 20:21 — And Edom refused *to give* Israel *passage* through his border.
   Isa. 37:28 — I know your *dwelling,* your *going out,* your *coming in,* yea, your *raging* against me.
   Syntactical summary: inf con as obj

3. The Genitive of Another Noun:
   Gen. 2:4 — In the day of Yahweh-God's *making* of heaven and earth.

2

cceles. 3:4 — A time of *mourning* and a time of *dancing*.
II Chron. 24:14 — Vessels of *serving*.

Syntactical summary: inf con as gen

In these instances translations use infinitives and gerunds to represent the infinitive construct. The ease with which English interchanges the two forms, often without apparent distinction in meaning, makes this a fitting thing to do.

4. Objects of Prepositions:

(1) With the preposition *le* (to):

le is used with infinitives construct very frequently. The variety of its meanings in these cases is such as to require painstaking discriminations.

In some cases *le* has lost its force as a preposition, as the English preposition "to" does in sayings like this, "To err is human, but to forgive is divine." The fact that we can say, "Erring is human, but forgiving is divine," shows that "to" has lost its force in this statement. In these cases *le* serves as a part of the infinitive itself.

In cases where *le* retains its force as a preposition, meanings like direction, specification, and relationship prevail. The idea common to all its meanings appears to be that of relation. It relates a verbal state to another fact that signifies its specific nature; it relates it to a purpose, result, or time toward which it is directed; or it relates it to a necessity toward which it tends, is intended, or is obligated.

a. As a part of the infinitive itself:

Gen. 4:2 — And she continued *bearing* (lit, to bear), even Abel, his brother.

Gen. 6:1 — When men began *to multiply* (or, multiplying) upon the face of the ground.

Gen. 11:18 — And so they gradually ceased *building* (lit, to build) the city.

Syntactical summary: inf con + *le* (obj of vb)

In translation it matters little whether we maintain the infinitive form or use a gerund. Frequently the two forms of expression are interchangeable in English without loss of meaning. Even when the infinitive form is maintained, we must look upon it as the object or subject of the verb; so it serves in the same way as the gerund. Therefore, these forms are grammatically the same as those under 1. and 2. above.

b. To show the specific nature of the verbal state:

> I Sam. 12:17 — Your evil is great which you did . . . *in asking* (or, *in respect to asking, with regard to asking*) a king for yourselves.
>
> I Sam. 14:33 — Behold the people are sinning *in eating* with the blood.
>
> Isa. 55:7 — For he will abundantly *pardon* (lit, deal abundantly *with respect to pardoning*).

Syntactical summary: inf con + *le* (sp nat of vb)

c. To show the relation of the verbal state to a *purpose toward which it is directed*:

> I Sam. 1:3 — He went up *in order to worship*.
>
> Gen. 1:17-18 — And so God proceeded to put them in the expanse of the heavens *to give light* . . . and *to rule* . . . and *to divide*. . . .
>
> Gen. 2:3 — Which God created *for making* (or, for the purpose of making, i.e., for development).

Syntactical summary: inf con + *le* (pur of vb)

"To" gives a neat expression of purpose when the context clearly indicates purpose. However, it is also used to express result. Because of this ambiguity, "to" is the fitting expression in many instances, inasmuch as it is impossible for us to know whether the author intended his infinitive to express purpose or result. When purpose is clearly intended, we can bring it out by using "in order to."

In Gen. 2:3, there is difference of opinion as to whether purpose or result was intended. BDB favors result.[2] Purpose is the interpretation given here, for the following reasons: (1) The whole story of creation is skillfully arranged from beginning to end to show that the process of making, i.e., development, was the will of God for all created things. (2) The infinitives in Gen. 1:17 which are selected by BDB as expressions for purpose,[3] appear to be parts of the long series of jussives and infinitives expressing this will or purpose of God. (3) This series of expressions signifying purpose is summed

---

2. Brown, Driver, and Briggs, *A Hebrew and English Lexicon of the Old Testament* (New York: Houghton Mifflin Co., 1906), p. 517.
3. *Ibid.*

up in these final words of 2:3, and thus it makes an adroitly drawn introduction to the "generations" or developments which follow, showing that sin was a violation of God's purpose for the moral development of mankind and that faith in God's purpose is essential to the salvation of the race.

d. To show the relation of the verbal state to an end or result toward which it is directed:

> I Kings 2:3 — And you shall keep the charge of Yahweh your God *so as to walk* in his ways, *so as to keep* his statutes.
>
> Judg. 5:18 — Who despised their life *to the point of dying.*
>
> II Kings 20:1 — Hezekiah was sick, *even to the point of dying.*

Syntactical summary: inf con + *le* (res of vb)

"So as to" is the most exact expression of result. In many cases, however, "to" and other variations will be suggested by the context.

e. To serve as a sign of direct discourse:

> Ex. 6:10 — And Yahweh proceeded to speak to Moses, *saying,* Go in, speak to Pharaoh.

After verbs of speaking, swearing, declaring, and the like, frequent use is made of the infinitive of *'amar,* to say, with *le* to mark direct discourse. The most probable explanation of this usage is that it originated as an indication of the result of the verb. However, it appears to be thought of usually as a mere sign of direct discourse.

Syntactical summary: inf con + *le* (sign of dir dis)

f. To show the relation of the verbal state to a necessity toward which it tends, is intended, or is obligated:

> Esther 8:8 — For the writing written in the king's name and sealed with the king's seal is not *to be reversed.*
>
> Isa. 6:13 — And if there remain in it a tenth, indeed it shall again be *for burning.*
>
> Prov. 19:8 — The one keeping understanding is *bound to find good.*

Syntactical summary: inf con + *le* (nec of vb)

g. To show the relation of the verbal state to a time approached by it:

Gen. 15:12 — The sun was *about to set* (near the time of setting).

I Kings 2:1 — And the days of David gradually drew near *to the time of dying.*

I Kings 18:29 — Then they continued to prophesy *until the time of offering* the evening sacrifice.

Syntactical summary: inf con + *le* (time of vb)

(2) With other prepositions related to time:

Josh. 3:14-16 — And it came to pass *during (be) the moving* of the people from their tents, *just before (le) passing over* the Jordan . . . and *at (ke) the coming* of the bearers of the ark to the Jordan . . . then the waters going down from above came to a halt.

I Kings 3:1 — And he proceeded to bring her to the city of David *until ('adh) finishing* the building of his house and the house of Yahweh.

Hos. 7:4 — Who is accustomed to cease stirring [the fire] *from the time (min) of kneading* dough *until the time of ('adh) being leavened.*

Syntactical summary: inf con + a prep (time of vb)

While many other prepositions appear with infinitives construct, there are no such problems in other cases as with *le*. Nevertheless, it is necessary to observe the distinctions between *le, be, ke, 'adh,* and *min* in reference to time. *be* indicates that the verbal state occurred in or during the period of time indicated by the infinitive; *ke* that it occurred at the point of time indicated by the infinitive; *le* that it occurred at a time before and near to, i.e., approaching the time indicated by the infinitive; and *min* that it continued from the time indicated by the infinitive.

Oftentimes it is fitting in translation to turn the adverbial phrases formed by these combinations into temporal clauses, substituting a conjunction for the preposition. Thus in Gen. 2:4, instead of saying, "in their being created," we may say, "when they were created."

(3) With *be* in a causal sense:

Ex. 33:16 — Is it not *by reason of your going* with us?

Ps. 46:3; 46:2 in Eng — Therefore we shall not fear *because of the upheaval* of the earth.

Syntactical summary: inf con + *be* (cau of vb)

(4) With *ke* in a comparative sense:

II Sam. 3:34 — *Like falling* before children of iniquity did you fall.

Syntactical summary: inf con + *ke* (comp of vb)

(5) With *min* in a causal sense:

II Sam. 3:11 — And he was not able any more to answer Abner a single word, *because he feared* him (lit, *on account of his fearing* him).

Syntactical summary: inf con + *min* (cau of vb)

(6) With *min* in a privative sense:

Isa. 5:6 — And I shall charge the clouds *not to rain* (lit, *from raining*) upon it.

In such cases the privative force of the preposition is equivalent to a negative.

Syntactical summary: inf con + *min* (priv of vb)

(7) With inf con + *ba'abhur* as an expression of purpose:

Ex. 9:16 — I have made you to stand *in order that I may show* you my power (lit, *for the sake of showing* you my power).

Syntactical summary: inf con + ba'abhur (pur of vb)

Chapter Nine

Means of Introducing Independent Clauses

The conjunction *waw* is the most commonly used means of introducing independent clauses. Its relation to these clauses needs careful interpretation. This interpretation needs to distinguish its use apart from verbs from its use with verbs. Certain other conjunctions used in comparative, disjunctive, and adversative clauses also need to be noted. *Waw,* however, is the only one whose use constitutes a problem.

The frequent use of *waw* where English prefers variety was not due to a lack of other conjunctions. The following observation concerning other conjunctions is quite pertinent: "Their frequent use was felt instinctively to be inconsistent with the lightness and grace of movement which the Hebrew ear loved . . . ."[1] The result of this instinctive feeling was the constant use of *waw* where English prefers variety and makes use of conjunctions like but, then, so, thus, therefore, that, and many others.

Only uses of *waw* as a copulative conjunction belong here. Instances in which it serves as a demonstrative adverb, meaning then and pointing to a specified time, do not belong here.

I

USE OF THE CONJUNCTION *Waw* APART FROM VERBS

There is an important distinction between the use of the conjunction *waw* to co-ordinate verbs and its use to co-ordinate clauses without being immediately related to the verbs by attach-

1. Brown, Driver, and Briggs, *A Hebrew and English Lexicon of the Old Testament* (New York: Houghton Mifflin Co., 1906), p. 252.

100

ment to one of them. In co-ordinating verbs it never draws an exclusive antithesis, but in co-ordinating clauses it may reflect an antithesis inherent in the clauses themselves.

In this connection BDB makes the following comment, "In such cases prominence is usually given to the contrasted idea by its being placed immediately after the conjunction."[2] As a result the conjunction is separated from the verb. No explanation of apparent exceptions is offered by BDB. It appears, however, that all exceptions can be removed, and rightly so, by translating *waw* as "and." Lev. 26:45 furnishes an example, as follows: *And* (usually translated "but") I will for their sakes remember the covenant of their ancestors. This verse appears to be correlated with the last statement of the preceding verse, "For I am Jehovah their God." If so, the meaning is *"and"* rather than *"but,"* and there is no antithesis. If the conjunction with correlative perfects is always handled as "and," then there are apparently no exceptions.

When we consider only those cases in which clauses, not verbs, are co-ordinated, we do find cases of sharp contrast, as in Gen. 2:17; 4:2. In these the meaning is "but." At times, as in Judg. 14:16, it introduces a contrast so as to suggest a question.

As seen in Isa. 46:4 and I Sam. 25:43, *waw* apart from verbs has an additive force as it does with them. In these cases the meaning is "and" or "and also."

Examples:

Isa. 46:4 — I made, *and* I will bear, *yea* I will carry so as to deliver.

I Sam. 25:43 — *And* also David took Ahinoam.

Gen. 2:17 — *But* from the tree of the knowledge of good and evil you may not eat.

Gen. 4:2 — *But* Cain was a tiller of the ground.

Judg. 14:16 — I told it not to my father or my mother, *and* shall I tell it to you?

II

CO-ORDINATING CONJUNCTIONS IN COMPARATIVE, DISJUNCTIVE, AND ADVERSATIVE CLAUSES

Comparison may be observed in clauses linked by *waw* conjunctive, as in Job 5:7. However, it is revealed in such cases by

2. *Ibid.*, p. 252, 1, e.

the obvious nature of the comparison, not by the conjunction. This fact is emphasized by the appearance of comparison in some cases when there is no conjunction, as in Job 24:19. It is permissable for us to make the comparison stand out by using correlative conjunctions like "as . . . so," but we should realize that we are imposing on the Hebrew sentence an addition to its original form and on the conjunction a meaning it could not have in the original form of the sentence.

When the Hebrew authors desired to cast a sentence in comparative form, they usually made use of *ka'asher* followed by *ken* as in the following:

Isa. 52:14, 15 — *Just as* many shall be astonished at thee —
So marred more than that of any man his appearance,
And his form more than that of the sons of men —
So shall he startle many nations.

At times *'asher* is used with the same force as *ka'asher* in these comparisons (cf. Ex. 10:6; 14:13; 34:18). Sometimes *ken* is used without its correlative conjunction being written, as in Isa. 55:1 and Jer. 3:20. In Eccles. 5:15, *kol-'umath she-*(in all points as) is used to indicate a complete parallel.

In disjunctive clauses the following are found:

Job 34:29 — *Whether* (*waw*) it is to a nation or (*waw*) to a man . . . .

Lev. 5:2-4 — *Or* (*'o*) if . . . *or* (*'o*) if . . . *or* (*'o*) if . . . .

Ex. 19:13 — No hand shall touch it . . . indeed he shall surely be stoned *or* (*'o*) shot through, *whether* (*'im*) it be beast *or* (*'im*) man.

Josh. 17:16 — *Both to* (*la-*) those who are in Bethshean *and to* (*wela-*) those who are in the valley of Jezreel.

Gen. 24:44 — *Both* (*gam*) drink thou, *and also* (*wegam*) for thy camels I shall draw.

Gen. 21:26 — *Neither* (*wegam . . . lo'*, lit, and also . . . not) did you tell me, *nor* (*wegam . . . lo'*) did I hear of it except today.

These examples show that *'o*, or, is the conjunctive naturally adapted to an exclusive antithesis.

In adversative statements the following are found:

I Sam. 8:19 — So they proceeded to say, No! *but* (*ki'im*) there will be a king over us.

Gen. 18:15 — So he proceeded to say, No! *but* (*ki*, without *'im*) you did laugh.

III

Uses of *Waw* with Verbs

The meaning of the conjunction *waw,* when attached to verbs, is very closely related to the meaning of the verbs themselves, particularly in the case of perfects and imperfects.   Superficial evidence appears in the great frequency with which this conjunction is attached to verbs, the different forms it assumes with verbs, and the effect of the combinations on the sentence.   Our preceding studies of verbs have laid a foundation for the study of this relationship, and here the combinations will be considered.

There are two forms of *waw* as a conjunction with verbs.   The simple form, usually written with *shewa,* is called *waw* conjunctive.   The special form, usually written with *pathah* and followed by *daghesh forte,* is called *waw* consecutive.

The relation of *waw* conjunctive and *waw* consecutive to the verbs to which they arc attached is so close that there appears to be a very sharp distinction between the combinations using *waw* conjunctive and the combinations using *waw* consecutive. When considered from the viewpoint of the distinctive character of perfects and imperfects, these combinations become the major problem in the syntax of biblical Hebrew.

As a fundamental distinction between *waw* conjunctive and *waw* consecutive, the following interpretations are offered:

(1) *Waw* conjunctive appears always to indicate a parallel. It is the only form of *waw* used with correlative perfects, and this usage magnifies the parallel.   With imperfects the relation may be co-ordinate or collateral, but it is still parallel.   A subordinate reason clause is collateral.   A graph may be formed by parallel lines with a brace at their ends to represent the conjunction.   (==================}).

(2) *Waw* consecutive appears always to indicate a sequence. It is the only form of *waw* used with consecutive imperfects. The relation between the imperfects linked by it may be temporal sequence, logical consequence, logical cause, or logical contrast.   In all cases there is a sequence.   A graph may be formed by consecutive lines with a brace at their juncture to represent the conjunction (———— } ————).

The exact contrast in meaning between these two forms of *waw* suggests that the difference in form was intentionally conceived as a means of indicating the difference in meaning.

Theories concerning the use and meaning of *waw* consecutive have differed from the interpretations given in this work at so many vital points that it will be necessary to examine these theories thoroughly. Then it will be possible to give a treatment of *waw* consecutive in accord with the treatment of indicative imperfects given previously in this work. Because a special feature of *waw* conjunctive is its use with correlative perfects, and because correlative perfects can be understood best in light of their contrast with consecutive imperfects, all combinations using *waw* conjunctive will be treated after treatment of those using *waw* consecutive.

1. Former Theories of *Waw* Consecutive:

The distinction between *waw* conjunctive and *waw* consecutive drawn above contradicts former interpretations in several ways. It is well, therefore, to note these contradictions and also the primary reasons for objecting to the old theories. Afterwards the positive interpretations of *waw* will furnish the fundamental argument against the old theories, inasmuch as they leave no place for the old theories.

The points of contradiction are as follows: (1) Whereas the old theories have said that there is a *waw* consecutive with perfects, this interpretation sees no such thing; (2) whereas the old theories have said that *waw* consecutive with perfects made those perfects the consequence of a preceding imperfect or its equivalent, this interpretation sees in every perfect a distinctive meaning arising from the fundamental character of all perfects; (3) whereas the old theories have suggested that the shift of accent on some perfects when *waw* is attached is a sign that the *waw* is a *waw* consecutive, this interpretation suggests that these shifts of accent are due to the grouping of words and syllables rather than changes of meaning; (4) whereas the old theories have said that *waw* consecutive with imperfects made those imperfects the consequence of a preceding perfect, giving them the force of perfects and virtually turning them into perfects, this interpretation sees in every imperfect a distinctive meaning arising from the fundamental character of all imperfects.

Primary reasons for objecting to the old theories are as follows: (1) The theory that perfects are used with the force of imperfects and *vice versa* is contrary to all reasonable expectations. Normal and correct developments in all other languages tend toward a discriminating usage that forbids substitution of one verb form for another.

(2) The fact that no special form of the conjunction appears with the perfect as it does with the imperfect is ground for doubt that a change in the fundamental meaning of the conjunction with the perfect was ever intended by the Hebrew authors.

(3) The theory that "the external indication" of a *waw* consecutive with a perfect "is to be found in the *alteration of the tone* which constantly attends and accompanies it"[3] is not supported by sufficient evidence. In explaining his conclusion, Driver describes it as a "conjecture."[4] In his discussion of the theory Harper makes this comment: "As a matter of fact, the cases in which there is no change of tone are as numerous as those in which there does occur change."[5] We may add that this great number of exceptions is not peculiar to parts of the Bible or certain authors but typical of all. If the one "external evidence" is lacking in approximately half the alleged cases, is not the burden put upon the subjective interpretation of the reader an overwhelming one?

(4) Advocates of the theory admit that there are constructions with *waw* for which the theory offers no explanation. Driver says, "The instances which occur must simply be recorded as *isolated irregularities,* of which no entirely adequate explanation can be offered."[6] In a footnote on the same page he adds ": . . in view of the number of instances it can scarcely be maintained with Stade that all examples found in pre-exilic passages are due to corruption of the text."[7]

(5) The theory defines no clear method of determining the force of the verb with *waw*. Driver says, "Whatever . . . be the shade of meaning borne by the first or 'dominant verb,' the perfect following . . . assumes it too: be the dominant verb a jussive, frequentative, or subjunctive, the perfect is virtually the same."[8] The word *virtually,* however, is made to cover a

3. S. R. Driver, *Hebrew,* (3rd ed., Oxford: The Clarendon Press, 1892), p. 115.

4. *Ibid.,* p. 118.

5. W.R. Harper, *Elements of Hebrew* (New and Revised Edition by J. M. Powis Smith. New York: Charles Scribner's Sons, 1921), p. 104.

6. S. R. Driver, *op. cit.,* p. 161.

7. *Ibid.*

8. *Ibid.,* p. 118.

strange mass of tangled ideas. It is true, of course, that in most cases translation can make the perfect with *waw* appear virtually the same as the dominant verb, but there are many in which it cannot. Harper cites perfects following imperfects with *waw* consecutive and gives to the perfects the force of a "frequentative imperfect." He cites other perfects following perfects and gives to them the force of "an ordinary future imperfect." He cites other perfects following perfects and makes the latter ones "imperatives." He cites other perfects in conditional sentences following "a participle, an infinitive, a finite verb (Perf. or Impf.), or a noun"[9] and makes them into imperatives. Where then is there a standard that can be consistently followed? Comparison of current English translations, the AV (1611), the ERV (1885), the ASV (1901), Moffatt's NT (1922), the Smith-Goodspeed AT (1939), and the RSV (1952), will show that the authors had not found one. Examples have been given in the preceding study of verbs.

(6) The confusion that prevails in the minds of students of the old theory is evidence that its logic is not merely so baffling as to overwhelm the majority of students but actually unsound. The most zealous ones, those who try to apply the theory to the Old Testament text as a whole, find themselves constantly vexed by confusing inconsistencies to which an application of the theory leads in translation. The distaste for Hebrew among theological students, growing largely out of an impression that it cannot really be understood, and leading 90 percent or more to drop it as soon as school requirements are met, appears to be attributable to the confusion arising from this theory more than any other single factor in the problem.

(7) The uncertainty persisting in the minds of the chief advocates of the theory is yet stronger evidence that their conclusions were based on weak foundations.

The unending search for a satisfactory explanation of this special function of *waw* has stood for more than a century as evidence of this uncertainty. It has been steadily pressed but not concluded ever since Bottcher in 1827 suggested that *waw* consecutive would be a better description of this special function than *waw* conversive. *Waw* conversive or *waw hippukh*

9. W. R. Harper, *Elements of Hebrew Syntax* (New York: Charles Scribner's Sons, 1888), p. 78.

had been inherited from Jewish grammarians of the tenth century and handed on without critical examination by Christian grammarians like Johan Reuchlin (1506), John Buxtorf (1615), and N. G. Schroeder (1792). Schroeder did suggest the need for interpretation by describing an imperfect with the special *waw* as *futurum relativum*, thereby suggesting that it was future by reason of its relation to something else. Since then the possibilities of this special function of *waw* have been examined at length by such men as Wilhelm Gesenius (1815), Heinrich Ewald (1827), A. B. Davidson (1878), August Muller)1882), W. R. Harper (1888), S. R. Driver (1892), and E. Kautzsch (1909). Nevertheless, their own words reveal again and again that they themselves remained conscious of serious questions left unanswered. A typical example is this statement of E. Kautzsch:

> It is difficult to give a proper explanation of this phenomenon . . . when we have given up the theory of a special *waw conversivum* in the unscientific sense mentioned in 49 b, note, at the end, and if we accept the fact that the *perfect* and *imperfect consecutive* cannot possibly be used in a way which contradicts their fundamental character as described in Pars. 106 and 107 . . . . The simplest view is to suppose that the use of the *perfect consecutive* originated from those cases in which it had to express the conclusion (or final consequence) of an action which was continued (or repeated) *in past time,* and that this use was afterwards extended to other cases, in which it had to represent the temporal or logical consequence of action, etc., still in progress, and thus in the end a regular interchange of the two tenses became recognized.[10]

The fact that Jewish scholars have remained as much in doubt about this matter as Gentile scholars has been shown by Dr. H. Leo Eddleman. Dr. Eddleman learned modern Hebrew in Palestine among Hebrew-speaking Jews; and he says, "In modern Palestinian Hebrew practically all scholars, influenced largely by their Occidental background, call *waw* consecutive *waw hammehappecheth,* which is equivalent to *waw hippukh* (*waw* conversive). Typical of these is Dr. Menaham Naor of the Hebrew University, Jerusalem, who says, 'There is [the method] whereby in our speaking of several actions, which occurred in the past, we put the first verb only in the past tense

---

10. E. Kautzsch, *Gesenius' Hebrew Grammer* (28th ed., Oxford: The Clarendon Press, 1910), p. 330, footnote.

and the verbs coming after it we put in the future tense, however, we join to them the *Waw* which changes them from future to past.' These grammarians do not, however, apply this same function of *Waw* to the case of a series of Perfects with when following an Imperfect."[11]

The reference of Dr. Eddleman to a difference made by modern Jewish grammarians in their interpretation of the function of *waw* with perfects and imperfects indicates a struggle in their minds over the very problems magnified in this work. While as far as we know no treatment of the whole matter has been produced by them, the evidence of an effort in that direction is significant. It indicates a sense of need in minds most conversant with Hebrew for a more adequate explanation of the ancient usage than has hitherto been given.

2. Uses of Waw Consecutive in Co-ordination:

In the case of *waw* consecutive and any imperfect to which it is attached, it is well to look at the relationship from the viewpoint of the verb. Thus viewed, the relationship is that of temporal sequence, logical result, logical cause, or logical contrast, i.e., the *waw* makes the verb to which it is attached to be a temporal sequence, a logical result, a logical cause, or a logical contrast of the verb preceding. Sometimes, as in Gen. 22:7, there are sequences parallel to each other. However, these follow a common antecedent and each is a sequent of that antecedent.

Waw consecutive is used only with indicative imperfects. Thus the sequence of *waw* consecutive and the progressive or frequentative force of the imperfect form a combination especially adapted to the description of lineal relationship. This idiom is thus distinguished at all times from those using *waw* conjunctive and describing parallel relationship.

Examples show that consecutive imperfects are not dependent upon any particular kind of antecedent. They abound in past time, and they frequently follow perfects; but this is not necessarily so even in narrative, as Gen. 2:6, 7; Ex. 15:1; I Kings 3:16; 8:1, 2 will show. (Evidence of consecution arises solely out of the combination of the imperfect with *waw* consecutive.) Thus the imper-

11. H. Leo Eddleman, "*Waw* Consecutive and the Consecution of Tenses as Reflected by Eighth Century Hebrew" (unpublished manuscript, Southern Baptist Theological Seminary, Louisville, Kentucky), p. 25.

fect with *waw* consecutive forms an idiom as independent and meaningful as the perfect with *waw* conjunctive.

Translation of the *waw,* however, must depend upon the logical relation of the constructions it links together. This is true with all forms of *waw;* it is particularly so with *waw* consecutive because the distinctions are many and sharp. Hebrew minds preferred to leave more to the interpretation of the reader than we do. In English we must insist upon translations of *waw* consecutive like the following:

Temporal sequence: also, and, likewise, then, afterwards.

Logical result: so, therefore, thus, hence, accordingly, consequently.

Logical cause: for, because, since, inasmuch.

Logical contrast: but, yet however, nevertheless, still.

  (1) To indicate a temporal sequence:

  Gen. 1:1-3 — In the beginning God created the heavens and the earth. . . . *Afterwards* God *proceeded to say,* "Let light come into existence"; so light began to be [i.e., on the earth. cf. v. 2].

  Gen. 6:9, 10 — Noah was (nar pf) a righteous man; perfect was he (nar pf) among his contemporaries; with God Noah walked (nar pf). *And* Noah *proceeded to beget* three sons.

  Gen. 2:6, 7 — And a mist proceeded to go up from the earth (prog imp), and it watered (cor pf) all the face of the ground, *then* Yahweh *proceeded to form* the man of dust from the ground, *then to breathe* into his nostrils the fulness of the breath of life.

  (2) To indicate a logical result:

  Gen. 2:7b — . . . then to breathe into his nostrils the fulness of the breath of life; *so* the man *became* a living creature.

  Gen. 3:6-16 — Then the woman began to observe that the tree was good for good, and . . ., and . . . ; *so she proceeded to take* some of its fruit, *and to eat, and to give* also to her husband with her, *and he to eat. Thus came to be open* the eyes of both of them, *and they to know* that they were naked, *and to sew* together fig leaves, *and to make* for themselves girdles. Then (tem seq) they began to hear the voice of Yahweh God walking in the garden at the breezy time of the day; *so they proceeded to conceal themselves,* the man and his wife, from the face of Yahweh God in the midst of the trees of the garden.   And (tem seq) Yahweh God continued to call to the man and (tem seq) to say, Where are you? *So he proceeded to say,* Your voice I heard in the garden; *therefore I became afraid,* for naked was I; *so I proceeded to conceal myself.*

(3) To indicate a logical cause:

(Use of *waw* consecutive to introduce a cause or reason clause is subordination rather than co-ordination.   Section (3), however, is included here to give the student opportunity to observe the similarity in construction.   See Cause and Reason Clauses later.)

II Sam. 14:5 — Of a truth *I am a widow, for* my husband *passed away.*

Ex. 2:10 — And she *began to call* his name Moses, *because she was in the habit of saying,* Indeed from the water I drew him.

Isa. 53:1, 2 — *Who* can *believe* our report? . . . *for he will grow up as a tender plant* before him.

(4) To indicate a logical contrast:

I Sam. 10:27 — And *the children of Belial* [worthless ones] *said,* How can this one save us?; so they proceeded to despise him, *and they did not bring* him *a gift; but he continued to be as a dumb man.*

Deut. 4:33 — Has a people *heard the voice of God* speaking out of the midst of the fire, as you heard it, *yet continued to live?*

Isa. 5:2 —And (tem seq) he proceeded to dig it and (tem seq) to gather its stones and (tem seq) to plant it with choice vines and (tem seq) to build a tower in the midst of it, and even a winepress he chiseled out (nar pf) in it, for he began to anticipate (log cau) the production of grapes: *nevertheless it brought forth rotten fruit* (lit, stinking things).

(Conclusion) Characteristic of Narrative:

Waw consecutive is the characteristic feature of all narrative. The narrative will begin, as a rule, with a perfect, as in Gen. 1:1, then shift to an imperfect with *waw* consecutive, as in

Gen. 1:3, in order to indicate a sequence between the verbal states. It may at any time, for emphasis, thrust words between the conjunction and a certain verb, letting that verb return to the perfect state. Soon, however, it will return to the *waw* consecutive with an imperfect in order to pick up the chain of sequences. Within the sentences introduced by *waw* consecutive, all kinds of varying constructions may appear, but always the narrative will return to *waw* consecutive to indicate movement from one event to another, one state to another, and so on and on so long as it is the wish of the author to continue his narrative. No matter whether the narrative be history, parable, story, legend, myth, or some other type of literary narrative, this is the manner of its composition.

Waw consecutive, therefore, is a major feature of Hebrew syntax. Accordingly, its recognition, its interpretation, and its distinction from all other conjunctive forms are exceedingly important.

3. Use of *Waw* Conjunctive in Co-ordination:

In order to maintain the same viewpoint at all times, we look at the relationship indicated by *waw* conjunctive from the viewpoint of the verb which follows it. Thus viewed the relationship is co-ordinate, correlative, or subordinate; i.e., the *waw* co-ordinates, correlates, or subordinates the verb to which it is attached with or to the verb preceding.

At times the relation is merely temporal, indicating simultaneous existence; at times it is also logical, indicating synonymous meaning; and in both cases there is a co-ordinate parallel, the two verbal states being made for the time being to enjoy equal rank and order.

As a rule imperfects, participles, and imperatives are co-ordinated with others of their own kind, with state, time, and mood being the same. The only variation that appears is the linking of cohortatives and jussives expressing polite commands and suggestions with imperatives expressing out-and-out commands. The co-ordination of clauses wherein verbs are separate from *waw* and assume wide dissimilarity, as in Isa. 46:4, is not in question here. Thus it appears that similarity of state, time, and mood is essential to such close co-ordination of verbs as is indicated by the attachment of *waw* to one of them.

The translation "and" seems to fit all cases, except those in

which repetition in the verbal idea calls for the strengthening of
"and" by the asseverative force of "yea."

(1) To co-ordinate indicative imperfects:

Isa. 40:30 — Even youths *will faint and be weary,* and
young men will utterly fall.

(2) To co-ordinate participles:

I Kings 3:3 — . . ., except that he *was sacrificing and
burning incense* in the high places.

(3) To co-ordinate subjunctive imperfects:

Jer. 31:37 — If the heavens above *can be measured and*
the foundations of the earth beneath *can be searched
out,* . . .

(4) To co-ordinate cohortative imperfects:

Gen. 50:50 — Now therefore *let me go up, I* pray, and
let me bury my father, . . .

(5) To co-ordinate jussive imperfects:

Gen. 1:6 — *Let there be* an expanse in the midst of the
waters, yea *let there be* a dividing of the waters . . . .

(6) To co-ordinate imperatives:

Amos 5:15 — *Hate* evil *and love* good *and establish* justice.

(7) To co-ordinate different states

I Sam. 28:22 — Now therefore, *hearken* (imv), I pray, to
the voice of your handmaid, and *let me put* (coh of req)
before you a morsel of bread; *yea eat* (imv), *and let
there be* (jus of sug) strength in you when you go in the
way.

(Perfects do not appear in this list because the co-ordination that is indicated in their usage is a stronger type of co-
ordination than that indicated in the case of other verbs. They
are linked by *waw* conjunctive to imperatives to show the details of the command, to the protases of conditions taken for
granted or sure to occur in general experience, and to central
statements in prophetic utterances to explain and expand what
the prophet says God will do for his people. Thus they introduce features of a preceding statement that are counterparts of
it, related to it logically by inherent and permanent co-ordination. This is correlation, and it will be observed in the next
section.

Combinations using *waw* conjunctive to subordinate one sentence to another do not belong in this treatment of independent clauses. A treatment of them will be found under Purpose and Result Clauses.)

4. Use of *Waw* Conjunctive in Correlation:

In all examples of correlation the conjunction retains the same parallel significance it has with co-ordinates. The verb, however, does not depend upon similarity to its antecedent for evidence of correlation. The antecedent may vary widely. The evidence of correlation appears to arise solely out of the combination of a perfect with *waw* conjunctive.

The parallel significance of *waw* conjunctive and the fixed nature of the perfect make a combination fitted to indicate that one state is a counterpart of another. The antecedent may present a general idea, while correlatives supply the details; it may give only a part, while correlatives describe other parts. In any case correlatives designate a state as a fixed part of a larger unit. The unity of the whole is the fundamental concept of this relationship. No matter whether the antecedent appear in a statement of fact, a conditional statement, a command, or an exhortation, details presented by this idiom fill out the picture and appear as fixed parts of it.

When a perfect is correlated with a frequentative imperfect, we naturally ask, "Is not the action of the perfect repeated as surely as the action of the imperfect?" For instance, if Gen. 2:6 is translated thus: "But a mist went up continually from the earth, and it watered the whole face of the ground," is it not indicated that the watering occurred frequently, even as the rising of the mist? Yes, it is so indicated, because the perfect with *waw* correlates watering with the frequent rising of the mist. Frequency is indicated by the imperfect, correlation by the perfect with *waw*.

An illustration in Ex. 6:6-8 is an outstanding example of this. There the statement, "I am Yahweh," is used like a sermon text. It is given in the beginning as the antecedent of all that follows, then repeated for emphasis in the middle and at the end. It is given as an assurance that God will fulfil his promise to bring Israel out of Egypt and back to the Promised Land. Accordingly, seven carefully correlated steps are itemized. In their midst an eighth correlative assures Moses that the people themselves will eventually realize that their God is Yahweh. Moreover, all of these steps are characterized as fulfilments which God will inevitably bring to pass by reason of the fact that he is Yahweh, God of faithfulness, righteousness, and redeeming love, able and determined to keep his covenants.

Another excellent illustration is that in Isa. 28:13b. There the prophet indicates that it is the purpose of Yahweh, in dealing with stubborn sinners who refuse all the aid of his merciful providence, to give them providential occasion for going on and on in their rebellion till they reap inevitable correlatives of reprobate character — falling backward, being broken, snared, and captured.

This idiom is so peculiar, yet its use so general and its interpretation so important in exegesis, that it challenges our best efforts to understand it. Careful comparison with the one which uses *waw* consecutive with the imperfect will help. In both cases a peculiar force is developed by reason of the combination of a conjunction and a verb with natures peculiarly adapted to each other.

Translation of the conjunction should accord with states that are counterparts of each other. "And" will give the mildest possible description of this close relationship; "then," "so," and similar translations will bring out the logical connection more forcefully. In most cases there is doubtless no occasion for stress; but in the apodosis of a conditional sentence, "then" is certainly needed.

Translation of the perfect should accord with its antecedent in time and mood. In the future, where the overwhelming majority of cases occurs, the auxiliaries "shall" and "will" need to be used always as an indication of the certainty expressed by the perfect.

Translators of the perfect have not hitherto recognized or stressed this relationship. Therefore, conflicting ideas such as contradiction have been unnecessarily read into it at times. In Gen. 47:30 a "but" has been put with the first correlative. Evidently this was done to make a contrast with the closing word of 47:29. That is unnecessary, because the closing word of 47:29 can be treated as a parenthetical statement. Moreover, the change has led to an artificial reconstruction of 47:30, adding "when" to the first clause and eliminating the conjunction in the second. If all correlatives in the two verses are treated as correlatives of the oath Joseph was asked to take, the Hebrew is clear. Another case of similar confusion occurs in Ex. 21:18-19. In all such cases we must look for a better translation, for contradiction does not accord with the nature of this idiom as seen above.

Such contrast as is expressed by "yet" or "still" does fit this idiom in many contexts. In these cases the conjunction indicates that, though a preceding statement is true, the one following is also true. This example in I Kings 8:27-28 is a good illustration:

Is it indeed true that God will dwell upon the earth? Behold, the heavens and the heaven of heavens *cannot contain* thee; how then this house which I have built: *Yet, thou shalt have regard* unto the prayer of thy servant . . . so as to hearken unto the prayer which thy servant is praying before thee this day.

(1) To correlate a perfect with a narrative perfect:

Eccles. 1:16 — Lo, *I magnified and increased* wisdom more than any one before me in Jerusalem.

(2) To correlate a perfect with an emphatic perfect:

Isa. 49:6 — *It is indeed too light* a thing for you to be my servant for raising up the tribes of Israel . . . *yea, I indeed give thee* as a light of nations, to be my salvation to the ends of the earth.

(3) To correlate a perfect with a previous-present perfect:

Isa. 1:2 — Children *I have made great and have exalted.*

(4) To correlate a perfect with a characteristic perfect:

Ex. 6:6-8 — *I am* [verb "to be" understood here, which would be *hayah* if written] *Yahweh, and I will bring you out* from under the burden of the Egyptians, *and I will rid you* of their bondage, *and I will redeem you* with an outstretched arm and with great judgments, *and I will take* you to me for a people, *and I will be* God to you, *and you shall know* that I am Yahweh your God, the one bringing you out from the burdens of the Egyptians, *and I will bring* you to the land which I sware to give to Abraham, Isaac, and Jacob, *and I will give* it to you as an inheritance: I am Yahweh.

(5) To correlate a perfect with a perfect of confidence:

Gen. 9:13-16 — My bow *will I surely set* in the cloud, *and it shall be* for a sign of the covenant between me and the earth; *and it shall be,* when I am bringing a cloud over the earth, then shall the bow be seen (pf + *waw* as a dem adv) in the cloud, *and I will remember* my covenant . . .; *yea,* the bow *shall be* in the cloud, *and I will look upon* it so as to remember the everlasting covenant.

(6) To correlate a perfect with an indicative imperfect:

Gen. 24:7 — *He will send* his angel before you, *and you shalt take* a wife for my son from there.

(7) To correlate a perfect with a participle:

Isa. 8:7 — Behold the Lord *is bringing up* against you the waters of the river, mighty and great, even the king of Assyria and all his glory, *and it shall go* up over all its banks.

(8) To correlate a perfect with a prophetic perfect:

Isa. 8:8 — And it shall sweep onward (cor pf) into Judah. *It shall overflow, and shall pass through;* to the neck it will reach (prog imp), and the spreading out of its wings shall be (cor pf) the fullness of the breadth of thy land, O Immanuel.

(9) To correlate a perfect with a subjunctive imperfect:

Isa. 28:13 — That *they may go on and shall fall backward and shall be broken and shall be snared and shall be captured.*

(10) To correlate a perfect with an imperative:

Ex. 3:16 — *Go and thou shalt gather* the elders of Israel, *and thou shalt say* to them, Yahweh the God of your fathers hath appeared to me.

(11) To correlate a perfect with a jussive:

Gen. 41:34 — *Let* Pharaoh *do* this, *and let* him *appoint* overseers over the land, *and he shall take* a fifth part of the land of Egypt during the seven years of plenty.

(12) To correlate a perfect with an infinitive absolute:

Isa. 5:5b — . . . *removing* its hedge *so that it shall be* for consumption and *breaking down* its wall *so that it shall be* for trampling.

(13) To correlate a perfect with a conditional statement:

Gen. 18:26 — *If I shall find in Sodom fifty righteous persons . . ., then I will spare* all the place for their sakes.

(Conclusion) Characteristic of Prophecy and Similarly Unified Composition:

Waw correlative is an outstanding characteristic of the composition used in prophetic utterance. Whereas narrative with *waw* consecutive attached to imperfects deals with the past, prophecy with *waw* correlative attached to perfects deals with the future.   Whereas the consecutive imperfects in narrative trace a series of sequences, the correlative perfects in prophecy describe the various details, or parts, or features of one central fact.   Whereas consecutives state facts of experience, correlatives state facts of faith.   This unique idiom is used in other important ways, but each one reflects the same characteristic feature seen in prophecy, i.e., unity with an antecedent.

After an imperative an author may use any number of correlative perfects to break down the original command into details.   If the author desires to issue an entirely different command, he continues with the imperative.

In dramatic portrayal of various phases of a scene, all occurring at the same time, an author uses these correlatives. See Ex. 33:8-11.   Within the sentences introduced by them, imperfects are used to describe movement and progress.   The several correlatives, however, present different aspects of one scene.

In conditional sentences correlatives appear in protasis and apodosis.   Always they are united with an antecedent.   In the apodosis, the entire protasis is the antecedent.

The vital significance of these correlatives in prophecy lies in the fact that they describe logical, not chronological relations. They provide no ground for chronological charts that attempt to reveal the time order of eschatological events.   They merely tie the great assurances of prophecy with the revelations, the promises, and the covenants of Yahweh God.

Chapter Ten

Means of Introducing Dependent Clauses

The types of dependent clauses are many. Because their natures vary so widely, the means of introducing them are many.

I

IN SUBJECT AND OBJECT CLAUSES

1. Subject Clauses:

Ruth 2:22 — It is good . . . *that (ki) you should go with his maidens.*

Eccles. 5:4 — It is better *that ('asher) you should not vow.*

In subject clauses it is customary to use *ki* or *'asher* as an introductory particle, *ki* usually, *'asher* less frequently. Even when serving thus as conjunctions, these particles appear to retain something of an old pronominal force. This is readily seen in *'asher* because it is regularly used as a substitute for a relative pronoun. Likewise *ki,* judged by synonymous particles in cognate languages, is thought to have originated as a demonstrative pronoun. These facts help us to understand that these particles sum up the meaning of their clauses, standing as it were in apposition to them, and thus they relate their clauses to the main verb exactly as a simple noun or pronoun used for a subject is related to the main verb.

2. Object Clauses:

Gen. 3:11 — Who told you *that (ki) you were naked?*

I Sam. 10:19 — . . . for you proceeded to say to him, *(ki) "A king shall you put over us."*

118

I Sam. 15:20 — And Saul proceeded to say to Samuel, (*'asher*) *"I have hearkened to the voice of Yahweh."*

Ex. 7:9 — If Pharaoh should speak to you, saying (*le'mor*), *"Present a sign on your behalf."*

Gen. 41:15 — I have heard concerning you, (*le'mor*), *"You can hear a dream so as to interpret it."*

Ex. 7:9 — And you shall say to Aaron, *"Take your staff."*

Ps. 9:21; 9:20 in Eng — Let the nations know *they are men.*

In object clauses *ki* and *'asher* are used as in subject clauses, except that they make their clauses objects rather than subjects of the main verb. In direct discourse they lose their force as conjunctions. They may retain the old force as a pronoun in apposition with the statement that follows, becoming equivalent to quotation marks, as in I Sam. 10:19, 15:20; but they are omitted at times, as in Ex. 7:9 and Ps. 9:21. Doubtless because of their omission, *le'mor* is used at times as another means of indicating a quotation. In some cases, like Gen. 41:15, we feel no need for translating it, leaving it as a mere sign of quotation.

II

IN RELATIVE CLAUSES

A relative clause is always related to some noun, either written or implied, in the main clause. Thus it partakes of the nature of an adjective, and the question of agreement with its noun is important. The relative particle *'asher* is nearly always used to introduce it, and sometimes the demonstrative pronoun *zeh* or *zu,* this. Since *'asher* is now a mere particle signifying relation, not a relative pronoun, a personal pronoun is usually brought into the relative clause to show agreement with the antecedent in person, number, and gender. The fact that the particle suffers no inflection at all makes it impossible for it to reflect such agreement. With the introduction of the personal pronoun, three essential points become involved in this indication of relation: (1) the antecedent, (2) the relative particle, (3) the personal pronoun.

In many cases, however, one or more of these essential points is not expressed, being merely implied. The translator must be prepared to fill in where English cannot bear similar abbreviation. In such cases, the identification of each of the three essential points with the other two becomes the key to the problem, as shown in the examples that follow.

1. With the relative clause written fully:

> Gen. 9:3 — Every moving thing *that is alive* . . . (lit, every moving thing which it is a living thing. . .).

The three essential points are as follows: (1) "moving thing" represents the antecedent; (2) "that" or "which" represents the relative particle (either English word may serve, since the antecedent is not a person); and (3) "it" in the literal translation of the original represents the personal pronoun.

The relative clause is composed like a substantive sentence; therefore, it has "is" for its verb, though the verb is not written in the original.

The personal pronoun is in the third person masculine singular; thus it indicates agreement with the antecedent. At the same time its apposition with the relative particle, which is the subject of the relative clause, marks the identification of the three and applies the description of the predicate "is alive" to all three. The identification is so close that it becomes unnecessary to carry the personal pronoun into the translation. The relative pronoun of the English, when substituted for the relative particle of the original, is quite sufficient to indicate the agreement. Retention of the personal pronoun would make the translation awkward.

An interesting fact appears in the translation of this relative clause into Arabic. It is reduced to one word in Arabic, and that word is an adjective. This interpretation reflects correctly the adjectival character of relative clauses.

> Gen. 24:15 — Rebekah *who was born to Bethuel* (lit, Rebekah who she was born to Bethuel).

The student needs to observe that the "who" of the literal translation stands for the relative particle of the original, while the "who" of the final translation is an English relative pronoun. Also let it be observed that the personal pronoun of the original, i.e., "she," is contained in the verb.

"She," being third person feminine singular, agrees with "Rebekah." It serves the same purpose as "it" in Gen. 9:3. When the relative particle of the original is replaced by the relative pronoun of the English, the need for "she" disappears.

> Jer. 28:9 — As for the prophet *who continually prophesies*

peace (lit, who he continually prophesies peace), by means
of the coming to pass of the word of the prophet will the
prophet *whom Yahweh has really sent* be known (lit, . . .
whom Yahweh sent him in truth).

In the first of these relative clauses, the personal pronoun is
contained in the verb of the original. It is necessary, therefore, to
understand as in Gen. 24:15 that the relative particle of the original becomes a relative pronoun in translation. Its inflection as a
nominative third person masculine singular agrees with "prophet"
and with "he." When this is understood, "he" is no longer necessary, for "who" becomes the subject of the clause.

In the second relative clause, the relative particle of the original
is not identified with the subject of the relative clause, i.e., "Yahweh," as in clauses already examined. It is identified with the direct object of the original, i.e., "him." When the relative pronoun
of the translation is put in the objective case to agree with "him,"
"him" has served its purpose and may be omitted.

Ruth 2:12 — . . . Yahweh, the God of Israel, *under whose wings
you have come to take refuge* (lit, who you have come to take
refuge under the wings of him).

In this clause the relative particle is not identified with the subject or the direct object, since the antecedent, "Yahweh," does not
serve as either of these. The phrase "of him," however, says that
the wings mentioned in the relative clause are his wings. This
phrase represents as construct, i.e., genitive, the relation between
"wings" and "him." In the English this genitive relation can be
indicated by the possessive case of the relative pronoun. When
the relative pronoun in the possessive case is substituted for the
relative particle of the original, "of him" is no longer needed.

Isa. 49:3 — . . . Israel *in whom I shall glorify myself* (lit, whom
in you I shall glorify myself).

Again the relative particle refers to an antecedent that is neither
subject or object in the relative clause. The antecedent, "Israel,"
is brought into the relative clause by the adverbial phrase "in you,"
with "you" as object of the preposition "in." When this preposition is put before the relative pronoun and the phrase "in whom"
substituted for the relative particle of the original, the need for the
phrase "in you" ceases.

In all these examples, the relative pronoun of the translation
takes the case the relative particle of the original would have if it

were a pronoun. For this reason it is necessary for the student, when reworking the composition of these clauses, to work out a literal translation including both the relative particle and the relative pronoun before he tries to put the translation in a finished form.

2. With the personal pronoun omitted:

Gen. 1:7 — . . . between the waters *which were under the expanse* (lit, which underneath with reference to the expanse). If the personal pronoun is added to this literal translation, the whole construction reads thus: between the waters which *they* were under the expanse.

As soon as the relative particle, "which," in the original is understood to have become the relative pronoun, "which," in the translation, it is not necessary to retain the personal pronoun, "they." All relations are clear without it. "Which," as subject of the relative clause is nominative. It does not change form as an objective identified with the antecedent, "waters," which is object after a preposition.

Gen. 2:8 — . . . the man *whom he had formed* (lit, which he had formed). Written with the personal pronoun added to the relative clause, the whole construction reads thus: the man which he had formed *him*.

Since the antecedent, "man," is the direct object of its verb, the personal pronoun, "him," is made the object of its verb. Then it is obvious that the relative pronoun to be substituted for the relative particle must be in the objective case; so we get "whom." "Him" is no longer necessary.

Gen. 35:13 — . . . in the place *where he had spoken with him* (lit, which he had spoken with him). Written with the personal pronoun added, the relative clause of the original reads thus: which he had spoken with him *in it*.

In the complete relative clause, the personal pronoun which is added, i.e., "it," is tied in by the preposition "in," so that the phrase "in it" indicates the place where the speaking took place. It also harmonizes with the phrase "in the place," of the main clause. When the phrase "in which" is substituted for the relative particle, it may be used as it is or turned into the conjunctive adverb "where."

Jer. 7:12 — . . . my place, *which is in Shiloh, where I made my name to dwell in the beginning* (lit, which in Shiloh, which I made my name to dwell there in the beginning). When a personal pronoun is written into each of these clauses, they read thus: which *it* is in Shiloh, which *in it* I made my name to dwell there in the beginning.

In the first of these clauses, all relations are settled like those in Gen. 1:7.

The second is almost exactly like that in Gen. 35:13. One difference appears in the fact that this one includes the adverb "there" in its original form. Therefore, when the phrase "in which" is substituted for the relative particle, it is natural to turn it into the conjunctive adverb "where" and to drop the adverb "there."

I Kings 8:47 — . . . in the land *whither they have been carried captive* (lit, which they have been carried captive there). With the personal pronoun added, the literal form reads thus: which *into it* they have been carried captive there.

The only difference between this and the preceding example is the fact that the verb in this case involves motion into or whither. Therefore, the conjunctive adverb that fits all relations is "whither" rather than "where."

Gen. 10:14 — . . . and the Casluhim, *from whom the Philistines went out* (lit, which from there the Philistines went out).

In this case the relative particle refers to "Casluhim," a people, while the phrase "from there" refers to the place of their abode. If both ideas are expressed fully, the clause will read like this: which *from the place of them* the Philistines went out.

"From whom" in the suggested translation uses the preposition "from" to signify a place and a going out from it. This phrase also uses "whom" to represent the relative particle turned into a relative pronoun and put into the objective case after the preposition.

In all these cases, due to the absence of the personal pronoun, the translator must deal with the relative particle as the representative of both. As a first step, he must observe the way the personal pronoun would fit into the clause, if used. Then he may transfer this personal pronoun or its entire phrase to the place of the relative particle. At the same time, he must substitute a relative pronoun for the relative particle and use its inflection as a means of integrating and abbreviating the whole construction.

3. With the relative particle, perhaps the personal pronoun also, omitted:

Gen. 15:13 — . . . sojourners will your descendants be *in a land that is not theirs* (lit, in a land not belonging to them). With relative particle and personal pronoun written, this literal form would be thus: in a land *which it* will not be theirs.

The relative particle "which" is turned into the relative pronoun "that." "It" is then unnecessary.

Isa. 42:1 — Behold my servant *whom I uphold continually* (lit, Behold my servant — I uphold him continually). With the relative particle inserted this reads thus: Behold my servant *which* I uphold him continually.

"Which" is turned into a relative pronoun and put into the objective case, in agreement with "servant" and with "him." "Him" becomes unnecessary.

Job 1:1 — There was a man . . . *whose name was Job* (lit, *Job his name*). With relative particle and personal pronoun added the clause reads thus: who the name of him was Job.

The relative pronoun, "who," can replace the personal pronoun, "him," if put in the objective case as object of the preposition, "of." The construct relation in "the name of whom" can then be expressed by "whose name," with the pronoun in the possessive case.

Ps. 16:3 — . . . even the excellent ones *in whom is all my delight* (lit, even the excellent ones — all my delight is in them). With relative particle added, the relative clause reads thus: which in them is all my delight.

"Which" becomes "whom" when made a relative pronoun and put in the place of "them." Then the phrase "in whom" is moved to the place of the relative particle.

4. With the antecedent included in the relative particle:

II Kings 10:5 — Therefore *he that was over the household* and *he that was over the city* . . . proceeded to send to Jehu (lit, who over the household and who over the city). With antecedent and relative pronoun written separately, these clauses read this way: he who over the household and he who over the city.

In both clauses, "who" as a relative particle becomes a relative pronoun in the nominative case, because it serves as subject of its clause. Then the verb "to be" understood needs to be written. Likewise "he," in agreement with this "who," is written into the main clause as subject of the verb "proceeded to send."

I Sam. 16:3 — . . . and you shall anoint for me *him whom I shall* name for you (lit, who I shall speak to you). When the antecedent and the relative particle are written separately, this clause reads this way: him who I shall speak to you.

When "who" is made a relative pronoun and put in the objective case as object of the verb "name," "him" is needed in the main clause as object of the verb "anoint." "Name for you" is a modern idiom equivalent in this context to "speak to you."

Gen. 43:16 — . . . then he proceeded to say *to him who was over his household* . . . (lit, say to who over his household). With antecedent and relative particle written separately this clause becomes: *to him who* over his household.

When "who" is made a relative pronoun, it serves as subject of its clause, and its verb needs to be written. Then "to him" is needed in the main clause to make all relations clear.

5. With antecedent, relative particle, and personal pronoun omitted:

When all points ordinarily involved in the indication of relation are omitted, it will be found that something in the main clause implies the antecedent. With the antecedent in mind other points can be discerned as in the examples under 3. In other words, the ways of indicating relation seen in examples under 1. are thought of as either written or implied in all cases, no matter how many omissions there are.

Ex. 4:13 — . . . send, I pray, by the hand of whomever *you will* (lit, by the hand of — you will send). With antecedent, relative particle, and personal pronoun written in, this entire statement reads this way: . . . send, I pray, by the hand of *him who you will send him.*

When "who" becomes a relative pronoun, it is put in the objective case to agree with the "him" of the relative clause. Then "him" is needed to complete the main clause and keep all relations clear. Since the use of "him" as both antecedent and personal pronoun makes its reference indefinite, it can unite with "who" in "whomever."

Job 18:21 — . . . and this is the place of him who *does not know God* (lit, and this is the place of — does not know God). Written fully this becomes: and this is the place of *him who he* does not know God.

When "who" becomes a relative pronoun, it is in the nominative case as an appositive of "he" and subject of the clause. "He" is no longer needed in the relative clause, but "him" is needed to complete the construct (gen) relation of "place" in the main clause. The relative particle with its entire clause served this purpose previously.

> Isa. 65:1 — I will let myself be consulted *by those who have not asked;* I will let myself be found *by those who have not sought me* (lit, have not asked; — have not sought me). Written fully and with the implication of the previous present verbs brought out, these clauses read this way: *by those* who they have not asked previously; by those who they have not sought me previously.

When the "who" in each clause becomes a relative pronoun, it is in the nominative case, being in apposition with "they" and the subject of its clause. "They" is no longer needed, but "by those" is needed in the main clause.

III

In Cause and Reason Clauses

Reason clauses usually cite facts already known to exist, as explanations of other facts. In these cases they point to actual causes. In other cases they cite definitely anticipated actions or situations, as ground for a warning or an exhortation. In these cases they point to strongly recommended reasons for actions, attitudes, or decisions. In all cases, the causes mentioned are thought of as definite and certain; so the verbs used are indicatives: perfects wherever the causes have already occurred or exist at the time of writing, imperfects if they are yet to occur.

The particles used to introduce these clauses accord with their nature. Some describe the cause or reason as that on which another fact is logically placed. These are: *'al,* on, upon, on account of; and *be,* in, on, by means of. Some describe the cause or reason as that from which the other fact proceeds as a consequence, a substitute, or an end. These are: *min,* from, as a result of; *tahath,* instead of, in return for; and *'eqebh,* as a consequence of, as an end of, due to. Some describe the logical accord or correspondence between the cause or reason and its consequence. These are: *ya'an,* answering to, corresponding to; and those combinations in which it appears with *ki* and *'asher. ki* and *'asher* are the particles whose origin was probably pronominal and which are used in a nominal sense to stand in apposition with the whole clause that follows. The pronominal particles follow the others when they are combined, and this usage is probably due to the fact that the others are thought of as prepositional in character. Sometimes *ki* and *'asher* stand alone in these clauses. They appear at such times to carry the meaning of the other particles with which they are often combined rather than a distinct meaning of their own. *Waw* consecutive, likewise, when attached to an imperfect describing a cause rather than a consequence as is usual with this combination, takes on the force of these characteristically causative particles. Thus it means *because* or *for*.

Ps. 119:136 — Streams of water run down from my eyes, *because ('al) they do not keep thy law.*

Amos 1:3 — (cf. 1:6, 9, etc.) For *('al) three transgressions, yea, for ('al) four,* I shall not turn it (i.e., the punishment) away, *even because of their threshing instruments of iron* (i.e., because they have threshed. . .).

Phrases with an infinitive and *'al* are frequently used to express a reason. They may well be expanded, as in this case, into clauses in the translation.

Deut. 31:17 — Are not these troubles come upon me, *on account of the fact that ('al 'ki) my God is not in my innermost being.*

II Sam. 3:30 — . . . so Joab and Abishai . . . killed Abner, *because of the fact that ('al 'asher) he had slain* Asahel.

Deut. 23:4, 5; 23:3, 4 in the Eng — An Ammonite or a Moabite shall not enter into the assembly of Yahweh, *because of the affair in which they did not meet you with bread and water ('al debhar 'asher).*

Jer. 3:8 — . . . *on account of all the causes in which ('al kol 'odhoth 'asher) a backslider, even Israel, had played the harlot,* I sent her away.

Gen. 39:9 — . . . neither has he kept back anything from me but you, *on account of the fact that (ba'asher) you are his wife.*

Isa. 43:3, 4 — *Because (ki) I am Yahweh your God, the Holy One of Israel, your Savior,* I give Egypt as your ransom, Ethiopia and Seba in your stead. *Since (me'asher, i.e., due to the fact that) you are precious in my eyes,* you are honorable and

I love you, and I continually give men in your stead and nations instead of your life.

Deut. 8:20 — . . . so will you perish, because (*'eqebh*) *you will not hearken.*

Amos 4:12 — *As a consequence of the fact that* (*'eqebh ki*) *I shall do this to you,* prepare to meet your God. . . .

I Sam. 26:21 — . . . I shall no more do you harm, *in return for the fact that* (*tahath 'asher*) *my life was precious in your eyes this day.* . . .

Prov. 1:28, 29 — Then they will call upon me, but I will not answer . . . *due to the fact that* (*tahath ki*) *they hated knowledge, and the fear of Yahweh they did not choose.*

Num. 20:12 — *Because* (*ya'an*) *you did not put your trust in me so as to sanctify me in the eyes of the children of Israel,* therefore you will not bring this congregation into the land.

Isa. 3:16 — *In answer to the fact that* (*ya'an ki*) *the daughters of Zion are haughty,* the Lord will smite. . . .

Deut. 1:36 — . . . to him I shall give the land . . . *in answer to the fact that* (*ya'an 'asher*) *he has wholly followed Yahweh.*

Gen. 3:14 — *Because* (*ki, in answer to the fact that*) *you have done this,* cursed are you.

Gen. 30:18 — *Because* (*'asher, in answer to the fact that*) *I have given my maid,* God has given me my hire.

Isa. 53:1, 2 — Who can believe our message? and to whom can the arm of Yahweh be revealed? for (*waw, waw consecutive of a logical cause*) *he will grow up before him as a tender plant* (lit, a little sucker, or a dependent plant) *and as a root out of dry ground.*

At times it is natural for us to take a co-ordinate clause introduced by *waw* conjunctive, as in Gen. 6:17; 22:12; Ex. 23:9; Job 22:12, and turn it into a reason clause with "for" as a conjunction. In these cases the clause introduced by *waw* states a fact that can be causally related to the first clause. The fact that the author used *waw* conjunctive means that he chose to leave discernment of the causal relation to the mind of the reader. If, however, the causal relation is clear, we do no violence to the text in substituting a causal conjunction and letting the clause be dependent. An instance in which the need for this interpretation is compelling is this:

Isa. 3:7 — I shall not be a binder up, *for* (*waw*) *in my house there is neither bread nor clothing.*

IV

IN PURPOSE AND RESULT CLAUSES

When an imperfect is linked with an imperative or cohortative by *waw* conjunctive, its mood appears always to be subjunctive and its relation subordinate.   The same is generally true when an imperfect is linked with any perfect or imperfect in the indicative. The only exceptions are rare.   For instance, in Isa. 46:4, where the last three verbs are imperfects in the first person singular and in future time, "I" is written emphatically with the first two; but with the third, even though it is expressing the same general idea, the emphatic "I" is dropped, and the verb is attached to *waw* conjunctive.   The explanation, apparently, is an intention to let the third express the purpose of the second.

This construction is used to express purpose or result.   In Hebrew, as in English, it is often impossible to distinguish between purpose and result.   If the preceding verb is an imperative or cohortative, purpose appears clearly, the voluntative force of the first calling for purpose in the second.   If the preceding verb is an indicative, it is hard to distinguish at times between purpose and result, but the prevailing effect appears to be result.

Translation should be varied according to the occasion for making the idea of purpose or result explicit.   When there is no occasion for making a distinction, "that" serves for the conjunction; when purpose is clear, "in order that" is better; and when result is clear, "so that" is the best expression.   In all cases the auxiliary of the subjunctive verb is "may" or "might," for past time, "may" to express stronger possibility in the present and future, "might" to express remote possibility in the present and future.

Examples:

Ex. 3:10 — And now *come,* I pray, *that I may send you.*

Ex. 4:18 — . . . yea, *let me return* to my brothers who are in Egypt *that I may see* if they are yet alive.

Lam. 1:19 — My priests and my elders perished in the city when *they sought food in order that they might sustain* their lives.

Num. 23:19 — God *is not* a man, *so that he may lie.*

Jonah 1:11 — What *shall we do* to thee, *so that* the sea may be calm for us?

In all cases cited *waw* conjunctive has served as an introductory particle. Other conjunctions that serve this same purpose appear in the following:

Gen. 12:13 — *Say,* I pray, that you are my sister, *in order that* (*lemay'an,* to the end that) *it may be well* for me.

Gen. 27:4 — And *make* for me tasty things . . . *so that* (*ba'ab-hur,* for the sake of) my soul *may bless* you before I die.

Either of the conjunctions in these last two verses is followed at times by *'asher,* that. Occasionally *'asher* alone occurs as the connecting word. In Eccles. 7:14, the phrase *'al dibhrath,* to the end that, serves the same purpose.

Infinitives construct with the preposition "to" (*le*) are used quite frequently to express purpose or result. The meaning is so very close to that of a purpose or result clause that it is expedient oftentimes to turn the phrase into a clause, making the infinitive to be a finite verb. The only suggestion concerning the distinction in meaning between the phrase and the clause is that the phrase is related to the antecedent verb in particular while the clause is related to the whole of its antecedent clause.

V

In Circumstantial Clauses

Circumstantial clauses describe circumstances which qualify, modify, or limit the verbal action or state. These circumstances specify the time, the place, the means, the manner, the limitation, or some other condition of the action or state described by the verb of the main clause. It is obvious, therefore, that they are related to their main clauses in the same way that adverbial accusatives and their phrases are related to simple sentences. All of them are adverbial. Thus the Hebrew naturally makes use of adverbs to introduce time clauses. The Hebrew usually omits all introductory words when using the other circumstantial clauses. This may be due to the fact that other statements concerning circumstances almost always employ an adverbial phrase rather than an adverbial clause. Apparently the only departures from this practice occur when *be* and *'odh* are combined to express continuance or *min* and *'odh* are combined for the same purpose. Since such words point to time as well as other circumstances, it is natural that full clauses be formed with them as with other conjunctive adverbs expressing time. Elsewhere, however, the introductory words are omitted, and it is necessary for English translation to supply those that fit the circumstances.

The conjunctive adverbs commonly used in the time clauses may be observed in the following:

Josh. 3:1 — . . . and they proceeded to journey from Shittim, to come to the Jordan, . . . and to lodge there *before* (*terem*) *they proceeded to pass over.*

Gen. 38:11 — . . . Remain a widow *until* (*'adh*) *Shelah my son will be grown up.* . . .

Deut. 2:14 — And the days . . ., *until* (*'adh 'asher*) *we passed over the brook Zered,* were thirty and eight years. . . .

'asher sums up the clause that follows as in various other kinds of clauses, but it does not appear to add to the meaning of *'adh*.

Lev. 14:43, 44 — And if the plague come again . . . *after* (*'ahar*) *he has taken out the stones,* then the priest shall come and look.

Ezek. 40:1 — . . . *in the fourteenth year after* (*'ahar 'asher*) *the city was smitten* . . . the hand of Yahweh was upon me.

Again *'asher* does not add to the meaning of the conjunctive adverb. Accordingly, English translations have ceased to add "that" to represent it.

Ex. 5:23 — . . . *since* (*me'az*) *I came to Pharaoh to speak in thy name,* he has dealt ill with this people.

Ps. 32:3 — . . . *when* (*ki*) *I kept silence,* my bones wasted away.

Isa. 28:4 — . . . *while yet* (*be'odh*) *it is in his hand,* he proceeds to eat it.

Num. 22:30 — . . . upon which you have ridden *ever since* (*meodh*) *you existed until this day.*

When circumstantial clauses appear without a conjunction, there may be some uncertainty concerning the exact nature of the circumstance. The two examples that follow will illustrate this fact.

II Sam. 18:14 — And he took three darts . . . and thrust them through the heart of Absalom, (*while*) *he was yet alive in the midst of the oak.*

"While" is not a part of the Hebrew text; therefore, the choice of it is a matter of interpretation. It is apt to be understood as indicating mere time, while the author may have omitted the conjunction to avoid that implication. He may have been thinking of the ruthlessness and cruelty of Joab and intending to emphasize the manner of this killing as another murder like that of Abner.   To bring out this phase of the matter one could translate thus: *with him still alive.*

Isa. 5:11 — Woe unto them that tarry late in the evening (*while*) *wine inflames them.*

Time is almost certainly involved here.   Either "while" or "til" may be used to express it.

The widespread use of phrases to describe verbal circumstances gives occasion oftentimes for the translator to expand these phrases into clauses.   The vividness of them may be more forcefully portrayed where it is possible to employ more words.   The following passage as a whole furnished an occasion for such expansion in certain phrases.   The phrases in question are these: "in the moving of the people from their tents" and "at the coming of the bearers of the ark to the Jordan."

Josh. 3:14-17 — And it came to pass, *during the time that the people moved from their tents for the purpose of passing over Jordan,* that the priests bearing the ark of the covenant were before the people.   *And at the moment when the bearers of the ark came to the Jordan,* then the feet of the priests bearing the ark were dipped in the edge of the waters, for the Jordan is full, over all its banks, all the days of Harvest.   However, the waters coming down from above proceeded to come to a standstill, they rose up in one heap, a great way off, in (a place called) Adam . . ., and the waters going down to the Salt Sea (the Dead Sea) were exhausted, they were cut off, and the people passed over opposite Jericho.   Therefore, the priests bearing the ark of the covenant of Yahweh continued to stand on dry ground in the midst of the Jordan, even securely, *while (waw) all Israel was passing over on dry ground, until (*'adh 'asher*) all the nation had finished passing over the Jordan.*

In verse 17 of the passage just quoted, in the clause introduced by "while," the Hebrew uses *waw* conjunctive, and the original clause is independent, co-ordinate.   Nevertheless, the clause describes a circumstance like the others observed in this section, and it is expedient to turn it into a dependent time clause.   Such occasion arises often.

It is also true that oftentimes an independent clause introduced by *waw* consecutive can be turned quite fittingly into a time clause.

An occasion of this kind arises whenever the first of two clauses, both introduced by *waw* consecutive, is used for the sole purpose of describing conditions pertaining to the time of the second.   Students need to remember that *waw* consecutive does not necessarily link its clause to the clause immediately before it.   The two clauses may be linked to a common source.   Thus Gen. 4:8 may be rendered this way:

> Gen. 4:8 — . . . *while they were in the field,* Cain proceeded to rise up against Abel his brother and to slay him.

The first clause, translated literally, reads thus: . . . and it came to pass, in their being in the field, . . . Each of these clauses has the first clause of verse 8 as its starting point.   Thus the first is used for the sole purpose of describing circumstances prevailing in the second.

This kind of construction occurs often in Hebrew, and the English translation is made much more attractive by the change, without any loss of meaning.

VI

TYPES OF CONDITIONAL SENTENCES

No sort of unanimity has existed among students of Hebrew concerning classification of conditional sentences.   Perhaps this has been largely due to lack of unanimity of opinion as to the nature of perfects, imperfects, and the conjunction *waw*.

In accord with preceding interpretations in this work four main types appear.   These four main types are comparable to the four that appear in other languages. This is doubtless due to the fact that the distinctions are rooted in logic rather than the idioms of any particular language.   These four main types are as follows:

(1) A condition *taken for granted,* i.e., one whose fulfilment is thought of as having already occurred.

(2) A condition *contrary to fact,* i.e., one whose fulfilment is considered impossible.

(3) A *more probable* condition, i.e., one whose possibility of fulfilment is taken for granted but whose actual fulfilment, in the case of an individual, is uncertain.

(4) A *less probable* condition, i..e, one whose possibility of fulfilment in any case and whose actual fulfilment are both uncertain.

VII
Verbal Sequences in Conditional Sentences

Type	Verb in Protasis	Verb in Apodosis
1. Taken-for-granted	Pf or pt Pre, prev pre, or prev fut Ind	Imp, pt, pf, or pf + waw Pre or fut Ind
2. Contrary-to-fact	Pf or pt with *lu* or *lule* Con subj Prev pa or pre	Pf or imp (with the force of *lu* or *lule* brought forward) Con subj Prev pa or fut
3. More Probable	Imp or pt Pre or fut Ind	Imp or pf + waw Pre or fut Ind
4. Less Probable	Imp Pre or fut Subj	Imp Fut Subj

Since each type uses particles and verbs which are signs of its own logical character, the particles and verbs of each type will be discussed separately. At the same time, there is a logical relation between protasis and apodosis in each type that calls for a careful consideration of their own relation in each type.

Type 1: Taken-for-granted:
(1) Verbs and Particles in the Protasis:
The condition stated by the protasis is expressed almost always by an indicative perfect, and occasionally by a participle, which is also indicative. Such verbs in previous present or previous future time present the condition as occurring previous to the time of speaking or previous to the time of the verb in the apodosis. Thus, for the sake of logical reasoning, they assume the occurrence of the condition, i.e., they take it for granted.

The particle used most often to introduce these conditions is *'im,* if. Occasionally, when the context shows that there is no uncertainty about fulfilment of the condition, this particle may be rendered seeing that, or when.

Another particle that appears quite frequently is *ki,* meaning if, in case that, supposing that, when, or though (when an adversative idea is expressed.)

Ki 'im, but if, or except, is used to present emphatically an exception to or limitation upon a statement already made. Cf. Gen. 32:27. (When the *'im* of this combination loses its force, as in Gen. 32:29, and its clause contradicts rather than limits the preceding clause, so that the resultant meaning is only a strong "but," its clause is co-ordinate rather than conditional. Cases in which the two particles are to be translated separately, as in I Sam. 14:45, also do not belong under this heading.)

Hen and *hinneh,* lo! and behold!, also appear occasionally. Practically they are the equivalent of *'im.* Cf. Gen. 4:14; Ex. 6:12; II Kings 5:20.

The particle of relation, *'asher,* in case that, or when, appears occasionally. Practically it is the equivalent of *ki.* Cf. Ex. 21:13.

In exceptional cases, the conjunction *waw* serves to introduce the condition. In these cases the conjunction is *waw* correlative, being attached to a perfect, and it ties into the clause it introduces the conditions stated in the antecedent clause. Cf. Gen. 33:13b; 44:22b.

It is possible for an author to depend upon juxtaposition and logical relation of protasis and apodosis to indicate what is the protasis. In such a case no introductory particle is written. Cf. Prov. 25:16.

(2) Examples:

Job 10:14 — If (*'im*) I indeed sin (pf in pre time), then thou dost mark me (pf + *waw* in pre time).

Ex. 1:16 — . . . if (*'im*) it is (pf of vb "to be" und but not written, in pre time) a son, then you shall kill (pf + *waw* cor in fut time) him.

Ps. 41:7a; 41:6a in Eng — And if (*'im*) he does come (pf in pre time) to see [me], he speaks falsehood continually (imp in pre time).

Job 7: 13-14 — When (*ki*) I say (pf in pre time), "My bed will comfort me . . .," thou dost frighten me (pf + *waw* cor in pre time) with dreams.

Ex. 8:17; 8:21 in Eng — But if (*ki'im*) you are not sending away (pt in pre-fut time) my people, behold, I will be sending (pt in fut time) upon you, and upon your servants, and upon your people, and into your houses swarms of flies.

II Kings 5:20 — . . . Behold (*hinneh*), my master has spared (pf in prev pre time) this Naaman the Syrian, in not receiving at his hand that which he brought; as Yahweh lives, most assuredly I will run after him, and I will take (pf + *waw* cor in fut time) something from him.

Gen. 44:22b — . . . The lad could not afford to leave his father; for if he shall leave (pf + *waw* cor in fut time) his father, then he [his father] shall die (pf + *waw* cor in fut time).

(3) Verbal Sequence:

The relation between protasis and apodosis appears to be strictly logical in all cases. *Waw* consecutive is never used; thus temporal sequence is ruled out. As a rule no conjunction appears in the apodosis; thus the very purpose of a conditional sentence to link a condition and a conclusion in a consistent statement is relied upon as a rule to indicate the logical relation. An imperfect in the indicative mood asserts the conclusion in the simplest possible way. A perfect in the indicative adds force to the assertion; a participle adds vividness. A perfect with a conjunction attached to it, in other words a correlative perfect, likewise adds force by use of the perfect, and in addition it makes explicit reference to the assertion by use of the correlative *waw*. This reference can be felt strongly, even in the "then" of English translations.

The verbal sequence involved in this expression of logical relation varies the state and time of the verbs but not the mood. An indicative in the protasis is followed by an indicative in the apodosis. Thus we observe that an indicative which asserts something as taken for granted in the condition calls for an indicative which does the same thing in the conclusion.

Type 2: Contrary-to-fact:

(1) Verbs and Particles in the Protasis:

Type 2, like Type 1, uses as its verb a perfect or a participle, usually a perfect, occasionally a participle. Unlike Type 1, however, it always uses an introductory particle. That introductory particle is either *lu* or *lule*.

Lu with a perfect or participle, as in this type, introduces a condition which the author knows has not occurred or which he thinks cannot occur. This particle with subjunctive imperfects carries an optative force in Type 4 but does not do so here. Here it marks its conditions as contrary to fact. It is translated if, but its meaning amounts to this: "If that which has not happened had happened, then the statement that follows would be true."

Lule', if not, except, or unless, is the opposite of *lu*. It is a combination of *lu* with the negative *lo'*, not. Through usage *lo'* has come to be pronounced as *le'*. It introduces a condition which the author knows has occurred, but which his statement describes, for the sake of logical reasoning, as not having occurred. This particle also marks its condition as contrary to fact.

It is essential to our understanding of these sentences to observe that it is the combination of the verb and its particle, not the verb alone, that indicates the contrary-to-fact nature of the condition. Alone these verbs would be indicative, asserting facts. The combination requires a classification of its mood as subjunctive, because it describes its condition as contrary-to-fact. The idea expressed is contingent, being dependent upon the thinking of the author for whatever reality it possesses. Thus it is subjunctive.

  (2) Examples:

  Judg. 13:23 — . . . if (*lu*) Yahweh had desired (con subj pf in prev pa time) to kill us, he would not have taken (con subj pf in prev pa time) from our hand a burnt-offering and a meal-offering.

  Isa. 1:9 — Except (*lule'*, if not) Yahweh had left (con subj pf in prev pa time) for us a very small remnant, as Sodom had we been (con subj pf in prev pa time).

  Deut. 32:27, 29 — Had it not (*lule'*) been (con subj pf of vb "to be," und but not written, in prev pa time) that I continually dreaded an enemy's provocation, lest their enemies should judge amiss, lest they should say, "our hand is exalted," then Yahweh had not done (con subj pf in prev pa time) this. If (*lu*) they had been wise (con subj pf in prev pa time), they would have proceeded to understand (con subj imp in prev pa time) this, they would have proceeded to look with discernment (con subj imp in prev pa time) to their latter end.

In verse 27a translators face a baffling puzzle unless they recognize the contrary-to-fact perfect of the verb "to be," which is understood as being there although it is not written, after the familiar pattern of simple sentences which use no written verb in asserting the existence of something. Without that verb "to be," the main verb in the protasis would be the indicative imperfect "I continually dreaded." That situation would violate all known usage in this type of condition. Recognition of the verb "to be" places a contrary-to-fact subjunctive perfect in the protasis, corresponding to another in the apodosis, found in verse 27d.

Another point of interest appears in verse 29. Imperfects are used in each of the two apodoses, as contrary-to-fact subjunctive imperfects.

> Ps. 81:14, 15; 81:13, 14 in Eng — If (*lu*) my people were hearkening (con subj pt in pre time) to me, Israel would walk continually (con subj imp in fut time) in my ways, in a little while I could subdue (con subj imp in fut time) their enemies, yea, upon their adversaries I would turn (con subj imp in fut time) my hand.

The participle in the protasis is a striking feature here. Again we find imperfects in the apodoses, three of them.

(3) Verbal sequence:

The logical relation of protasis and apodosis remains logically consistent. Though *lu* or *lule'* is not repeated in the apodosis, the purpose of a conditional sentence to link a condition and a conclusion in a consistent and unified statement is relied upon to show that the contrary-to-fact character of the protasis is carried over into the apodosis. A perfect in the apodosis states the conclusion in terms of one fixed action or state. An imperfect states the conclusion of progress or frequency. In either case the sentence as a whole indicates that the conclusion is contrary to fact.

The verbal sequence makes a contrary-to-fact subjunctive to follow a contrary-to-fact subjunctive. Verbal state and time varies, as in Type 1, but not the mood.

Type 3: More Probable:

(1) Verbs and Particles in the Protasis

Imperfects and participles appear in the protasis, imperfects regularly, participles very rarely. The perfect is not used, and this fact shows that this type passes from the fixed conditions of Types 1 and 2 into the realm of probability.

Both *'im* and *ki* are used regularly as introductory particles. *'Akh 'im,* but if, or if, however, occurs rarely with an adversative force.   All of these introduce conditions whose possibility of fulfilment in many cases is not questioned, but whose actual fulfilment in an individual case is uncertain.   Thus their conditions may fittingly be called more probable.   They are certainly more probable than those of Type 4, in which both possibility and actual fulfilment are uncertain.

In a series of conditions which employs both *ki* and *'im,* perhaps *'akh 'im* and the like, *ki* introduces a situation or factor common to all, while *'im* or any other introduces details and variations.   Thus *ki,* as a rule, introduces conditions more likely to occur than those introduced by *'im.*   Nevertheless, the context may add to the normal force of *'im* and make it to introduce a condition concerning which no uncertainty is expressed.   Thus Jacob, in Gen. 28:20-22, was accepting the promise Yahweh had just made to him.   Moreover, he was promising in turn to accept Yahweh as his God and also to pay tithes to him.   The promise about tithing was not bargaining, for Yahweh had already made his promise.   Jacob's promise was a response of gratitude and a promise of obedience.   Therefore, in this passage *'im* means "seeing that."   Likewise, in Num. 36:4, Isa. 4:4; 24:13; 28:25, *'im* means "when."

(2) Examples:

Mal. 2:2 — If (*'im*) you will not hear (ind imp in fut time), and if (*'im*) you will not lay it (ind imp in fut time) to heart, to give glory to my name . . ., then I will send (ind pf + *waw* cor in fut time) the curse upon you, yea, I will curse (ind pf + *waw* cor in fut time) your blessings.

Isa. 1:19, 20 — If (*'im*) you will be willing (ind imp in fut time) and shall hearken (ind pf + *waw* cor in fut time, adding to the description of the condition), the good of the land you will eat (ind imp in fut time). But if you will be unwilling (ind imp in fut time) and shall rebel (ind pf + *waw* cor, adding to the condition), by the sword you will be devoured (ind imp in fut time).

Gen. 44:32 — . . . if (*'im*) I shall not bring him (ind imp

in fut time) to you, then I will have sinned (ind pf +
waw cor in prev fut time) against my father forever.

Comparison of this verse with Gen. 43:9 is highly instructive.
In Gen. 43:9 Judah, while speaking to his father, anticipates the
same situation he does here, while speaking to Joseph.   However, in 43:9, he uses a condition taken for granted, while here
he uses a more probable condition.   In speaking to his father he
wanted him to think of the return of Benjamin as an event
taken for granted, so that he would let Benjamin go to Egypt.
In speaking to Joseph, whom he knew only as premier of Egypt,
he could not afford to take the condition for granted, yet he
desired desperately to impress him with the terrible effect a
failure on his part to assure the return of Benjamin would have
on his father.   For Joseph's sake he needed to picture that
failure as probable but not as taken for granted.   When he
went on to offer himself as a substitute for Benjamin, he indeed made a tremendous impression on Joseph.   In other words,
Judah recognized the fine distinction he made, and he felt the
force of it very deeply.   It was an exceedingly important matter
to him.

> Ex. 21:2, 5, 6, 7, 11 — When (*ki*) you buy (ind imp in
> pre time) as a slave a Hebrew man, six years will he
> serve (ind imp in fut time); and in the seventh, he may
> go out free . . . .   But if (*'im* with the conjunction "but")
> the servant says (ind imp in pre time) positively, "I
> love my master, my wife, and my children; I shall not
> go free," then his master shall bring him (ind pf + *waw*
> cor in fut time) to The [One True] God, yea, he shall
> bring him (ind pf + *waw* in fut time) to the door, or
> the door-post, and his master shall bore (ind pf + *waw*
> cor in fut time) his ear through with an awl, and he
> shall serve him (ind pf + *waw* cor in fut time) forever.

> And when (*ki*) a man sells (ind imp in pre time),
> his daughter as a house-hold slave, she will not go out
> as the male-slaves go out. . . .   And unless (*'im* + the
> negative) he does (ind imp in fut time) these three
> things for her, then she shall go out (ind pf + *waw* cor
> in fut time) for nothing, without money.

(Verses 3, 4, 8, 9, 10 are omitted here because their conditions belong to Types 1 and 4.   The last sentence in verse 2
is included because it prepares the way for the contrasting state-

ment in verse 5. Compare the treatment of the whole passage
below under Type 4)

(3) Verbal Sequence:

In type 3, indicatives in the protasis are followed by indicatives in the apodosis. This is like the sequence in Type 1.
Moreover, the indicative in the apodosis may be an imperfect
or a perfect with *waw* correlative. So far as Type 3 construction in the apodosis goes, it is exactly like that in Type 1.

Type 4: Less probable:

(1) Verbs and Particles in the Protasis:

Imperfects only are used in the protasis. Moreover, the conditions are described in ways that raise questions concerning
the possibility of fulfilment. Therefore, these verbs are subjunctive. They not only express uncertainty about fulfilment in
an individual case, but in any case.

'Im appears as the only introductory particle. In all cases
it means if, or though, never when, or seeing that, as it does
occasionally in Type 1 and Type 3.

(2) Examples:

> Gen. 13:16 — . . . if (*'im*) a man could be able to count
> (subj imp in fut time) the dust [particles] of the earth,
> also your seed [descendants] could be counted (subj
> imp in fut time).

> Jer. 31:36, 37 — "If (*'im*) these ordinances could depart
> (subj imp in fut time) from before me," is the express
> utterance of Yahweh, "also the seed of Israel could cease
> from being a nation before me forever." Thus doth say
> Yahweh: " 'If (*'im*) the heavens above could be mea-
> sured (subj imp in fut time), and the foundations of
> the earth could be searched out (subj imp in fut time),
> also I could cast off (subj imp in fut time) all the seed of
> Israel, because of all that they have done,' is the ex-
> press utterance of Yahweh."

> Jer. 33:20, 21 — If (*'im*) you could break (subj imp in
> fut time) my covenant with the day and my covenant
> with the night, so that day and night would not be in
> their time, also my covenant with David could be broken
> (subj imp in fut time), so that there would not be a son
> of his reigning upon his throne — and with the Leviti-
> cal priests my ministers.

Isa. 1:18 — Though (*'im*) your sins may be (subj imp in pre time) as scarlet, they may be made white (subj imp in fut time) as snow: though they may be red (subj imp in pre time) like crimson, they may become (subj imp in fut time) like wool.

(3) Verbal Sequence:

In the translations given above, subjunctive imperfects in the protases are followed by subjunctive imperfects in the apodoses. This feature of verbal sequence is thus presented as the essential characteristic of Type 4 conditional sentences. As indicatives follow indicatives in Type 1, that in the protasis being a perfect or participle; as contrary-to-fact subjunctives in Type 2 follow contrary-to-fact subjunctives, that in the protasis being a perfect or participle preceded by *lu* or *lule'*; as indicatives follow indicatives in Type 3, that in the protasis being an indicative imperfect; so subjunctives follow subjunctives in Type 4, that in the protasis being a subjunctive imperfect. The mere fact that there appears to be a pattern here that can relieve translations of a high degree of subjectivity is enough to challenge every student of the subject to examine this apparent pattern very, very carefully.

On the other hand, there is much, much variation from this suggested pattern in existing translations. This, likewise, demands examination.

As stated in the introduction to this treatment of conditional sentences, "no sort of unanimity has existed among students of Hebrew concerning classification of conditional sentences." This fact has been obvious and very disturbing. In view of the earnest effort throughout this survey to find a distinctive meaning for all verb forms, all conjunctions, all combinations of these, and all types of sentence structure, it follows therefore that another comment in the introduction is pertinent here: "Perhaps, this has been largely due to lack of unanimity of opinion as to the nature of perfects, imperfects, and the conjunction *waw*."

Accordingly, an attempt will be made in the section that follows to apply all previous conclusions to this exceedingly complex matter. An extensive passage, filled with conditional sentences from end to end, will be used as a basis for this examination.

VIII

A COMPARISON OF CONDITIONAL SENTENCES IN EXODUS 21:2-14

In the following passage conditions belonging to Type 1 and Type 3 are included along with those belonging to Type 4. This gives an excellent opportunity for comparison and for drawing certain important conclusions concerning the syntactical construction used for these sentences. Only in the conditions of Type 4 will a description of the verbs be included. This will be done to mark these conditions as belonging to Type 4 and to invite comparison with the other types in this passage.

Exodus 21:2-14:

2. When (*ki*) you buy as a slave a Hebrew man, six years will he serve; and in the seventh he may go out free, without paying anything. 3. If (*'im*) by himself he should come in (subj imp in fut time), by himself he may go out (subj imp in fut time); if (*'im*) he is married, then his wife shall go out with him. 4. If (*'im*) his master should give (subj imp in fut time) him a wife, and she shall bear (pf + *waw* cor, which merely adds to the condition a detail which assumes the same conditional force as the preceding verb) him sons or daughters, the wife and her children should belong (sub imp in fut time) to her master, but he may go out (subj imp in fut time) by himself. 5. But if (*'im*) the servant says positively, "I love my master, my wife, and my children; I shall not go out free," 6. then his master shall bring him to The [One True] God,[1] yea, he shall bring him to the door, or to the door-post, and his master shall bore his ear through with an awl, and he shall serve him forever.

7. When (*ki*) a man sells his daughter as a household-slave, she will not go out as the male-slaves go out. 8. If (*'im*) she is not pleasing in the eyes of her master, who has espoused her to himself,[2] then he shall cause her to be redeemed: to a foreign people he will not have power to sell her, because of his dealing deceitfully with her. 9. And if (*'im*) he should espouse her (subj imp in fut time) to his son, according to the judgment for daughters he should deal

1. Or, the judges.
2. Some mss. read thus: so that he has not espoused her.

(subj imp in fut time) with her.   10. If (*'im*) he should take (subj imp in fut time) for himself another [wife], her food, her clothing, and her duty of marriage he should not diminish (subj imp in fut time).   11. And if (*'im*) he does not do these three things for her, then she shall go out for nothing, without money.

12. One who smites a man, and he dies, may surely be put to death.   13. But in case (*'asher*) he did not lie in wait, but The [One True] God delivered [his enemy] into his hand, then I will appoint for you a place to which he may flee.   14. But when (*ki*) a man acts with premeditation against his neighbor to slay him with guile, from my altar you will take him that he may die.

Frequently in this passage and in similar passages wherever the ordinances are recited, other translations use a subjunctive in the protasis and an indicative in the apodosis.   Ex. 21:3 furnishes a good example: "If by himself he comes in, by himself he shall go out."   Imperfects appear in both in the Hebrew, and the translations make one subjunctive, the other indicative.

In searching for reasons why this has been done, a situation in the immediate context should be noted.   At the end of verse 2 there is a statement that introduces all the conditional sentences that follow from verse 2 through verse 6.   That final sentence is not a condition.   If the author had intended to put the statement in a conditional sentence, it would have served as conclusion rather than condition after this fashion: and if he should desire to go out free, he may do so.   As written it is merely a statement, preliminary to the several conditional sentences that follow.

In view of the logical relation between that preceding statement and the varying choices stated afterwards, it is not logically consistent to say "he shall go out free."   Various possibilities are stated below, and wherever an alternative choice is stated consistency requires an introductory statement that says "he may go out free."   The lack of logical integrity, when verse 2 says that the slave shall go out and verse 6 says that he shall remain forever, smites the mind of a thoughtful reader.

Since the verb in this introductory statement is an imperfect, it may be interpreted as subjunctive.   Then its auxiliary must be "may," not "shall."   (Even if it were interpreted as an indicative, it would not take "shall."   Only a perfect could do that.)

With the introductory statement in the subjunctive, a subjunctive statement of varied details given in protases is consistent. Apodoses in the subjunctive are likewise consistent. The logical consistency of these can be recognized easily in verses 3a and 4. Similar interpretations are called for in verses 9 and 10.

Instructive contrasts appear in verses 2a, 7, and 14. Imperfects are used in protasis and apodosis to describe basic legal practices. Apparently, this is indicated by the use of *ki* as the introductory particle. Thus "when" is required in translation. Thus the imperfects are indicatives, and the sentence is Type 3.

Other instructive contrasts appear in verses 5, 6 and 11. Imperfects are used in the protasis to describe particular situations in which the condition is so stated as to eliminate all alternative conditions. Naturally that imperfect is indicative. Then the apodoses use perfects with *waw*. Thus they not only give a positive, i.e., indicative, statement to the only conclusion allowed by law in that case but they state it as forcefully as possible.

Conditions using perfects or participles, but not with *lu* or *lule'* before them, fall into Type 1. After these conditions taken for granted, the use of a perfect with *waw* correlative in the apodosis is quite consistent. One example appears in verse 13.

Conditions with the same composition as substantive sentences, i.e., without a written verb but with the verb "to be" understood, imply such a verb in the indicative perfect. Thus they also belong to Type 1. Examples appear in verses 3b and 8a. In both cases a perfect with *waw* correlative is used in the apodosis. This usage emphasizes the sequence which requires the same mood in protasis and apodosis.

A correlative construction correlated with a subjunctive antecedent, as in the protasis of verse 4, assumes the conditional force of its antecedent, since it states a detail of that antecedent. It is then consistent with a subjunctive conclusion. In all cases where a correlative appears in an apodosis, as in verses 3b, 6 (four instances), 8a, 11, and 13, that correlative has an indicative in the protasis as its antecedent. All this magnifies the interpretations of verbal sequence as requiring the same mood in protasis and apodosis.

The use of perfects with *waw* in the apodoses of these sentences presents a body of evidence that is vital to our entire treatment of Hebrew syntax. The following points require this evaluation of its importance:

(1) The interpretation of these perfects with *waw* contains the same problem involved in perfects with *waw* anywhere else. Our survey has revealed no variation in the essential idea expressed by this construction, i.e., unity with its antecedent. Therefore, any variation in this situation is expected to be in the context of this particular construction, not in the construction itself.

(2) The interpretation of these perfects with *waw* has been baffling, even to the very best scholars in the field, and to a degree that is almost unbelievable until one examines the mass of conflicting interpretations given to conditional sentences in works on Hebrew syntax. Men who have been unable to accept the theory that the *waw* with these perfects is *waw* consecutive, and that it brings to these perfects the force of the verb in the protasis, in many cases an imperfect, have been forced into silence with little or nohing to relieve their confusion. Men who have accepted this theory have continued through centuries of effort to turn out translations with a woeful lack of consistency in them. The same inconsistencies noted above in the discussion of Ex. 21:2-14 appear in AV, ASV, MNT, AT, RSV, and in all commentaries, so far as the author is aware of them.

(3) The translation of Exodus 21:2-14 gives an excellent opportunity for weighing the force of perfects with *waw,* because conditional sentences of Types 1, 3, and 4 appear together with many occasions for comparison.

In verse 3b the first instance occurs, in these words, "and his wife shall go out with him." Since this conclusion deals with the wife in case of her husband choosing to go free, the one conclusion allowed by the law is stated very positively by this construction.

In verse 4a, this construction is in the protasis following a main verb, and it assumes the time and mood of that main verb. This fact illustrates the unity it expresses, but it affects the sentence as a whole in no other way than the addition of a detail to the condition.

In verses 5 and 6, which are parts of one sentence, the apodosis uses four of these constructions to describe the one conclusion allowed by the law. Again they do so with force, naturally so.

Verse 8a, like 3b, uses this construction in the apodosis to state very positively the point required by the law.

In verse 11, the protasis eliminates all conditions other than its own, then the apodosis uses this construction to emphasize the one conclusion allowed by the law.

Verse 13 is like 3b, with the same need for force in statement of the one conclusion allowed by law.

This translation uses the auxiliary "shall" to express the force of these perfects with *waw* wherever they appear in apodoses, and it does not use it in any other case. This distinction makes these perfects with *waw* to stand out, even as the logical consistency of all these sentences requires. This then becomes crucial evidence in resolving our problem.

In view of the consistency brought to this passage by consistent interpretation of its verbs, and in view of conviction that similar interpretation brings consistency to all passages listing ordinances, the pattern of verbal sequences described above is believed to be confirmed.

IX

MIXED FORMS IN CONDITIONAL SENTENCES

The sentences discussed in the foregoing have belonged to regular types. Conditional sentences are not always so regular by any means.

At times a condition belonging to one type is combined in the protasis with a condition of another type, as follows:

Isa. 4:4 — When (*'im*) the Lord shall have washed away (ind pf in prev fut time) the filth of the daughters of Zion, and the bloodguiltiness of Jerusalem he will proceed to purge (ind imp in fut time) from her midst by the spirit of justice and the spirit of burning, then Yahweh shall create (ind pf + *waw* in fut time) over each dwelling in Mount Zion and over her assembly a cloud by day, even a smoke-cloud, and a brightness of a flame of fire by night . . . .

The first condition belongs to Type 1, and the second to Type 3. The apodosis, however, which employs an indicative perfect with *waw,* fits both of them.

Conditions are frequently mixed with clauses that are not conclusions of a normal type. Frequently interrogative, imperative, cohortative, or jussive clauses appear in place of the normal statements we have observed. It is impossible to reduce such sentences to a system. The essential thing to remember in these cases is that each part of the sentence must be judged by the standards for its type of clause.

Oaths and imprecations belong to this group. Occasionally these are written fully, as in Ruth 1:17, but frequently the apodosis is omitted, no expression of any kind appearing in its place, as in II Sam. 11:11. Often a formal expression indicating an oath, like *chay Yahweh*, as lives Yahweh, will accompany the condition, but it does not furnish the apodosis. Probably the apodosis is understood to be in all cases the equivalent of that which is sometimes written: "The Lord do so to me and more also." The effect of such expressions is to convey the strongest possible impression that the thing in question will or will not be done. If the particle used is *'im* or *ki,* supposing the doing of it, the effect is to affirm that it will not be done, as in I Sam. 14:45. If the particle used is *'im lo,* if not, supposing that the thing not be done, the effect is to affirm the doing of it, as in Gen. 24:38. For the sake of clarity, the translation must often render the effect rather than the literal expression.

For the sake of clarifying some of these interpretations, certain examples will be examined more closely:

Ruth 1:17 — . . . so let Yahweh do (a jussive imp), yea, let him add [to it, i.e., destroy me], if (*ki*) death itself (lit, the death) can divide (subj imp in fut time) between me and you.

The condition is stated last. Ruth's words appear to express conviction that death itself cannot put an actual or permanent barrier between them. There is no word like "only" or "aught but" among her words.

II Sam. 11:11 — . . . as you live, and as your soul lives, [let Yahweh destroy me, an unexpressed jus imp, serving as the apodosis], if (*'im*) I shall do (ind imp in fut time) this thing.

The clauses "as you live" and "as your soul lives" were idioms that signified the taking of an oath. They did not state the conclusion, but they prepared the mind of the hearer to realize that the customary conclusion was desired by the speaker as surely as if it had been spoken.

I Sam. 14:45 — . . . as Yahweh lives, [let Yahweh destroy us, a jus imp expressing the conclusion] if (*'im*) one hair of his head (lit, from the hair of his head) will fall (ind imp in fut time) to the ground.

The effect of this dramatic oath is to swear that no hair of his head will fall to the ground.

Gen. 24:38 — If not (*'im lo'*) to the house of my father you will go, and to my family, and you shall take (cor pf in fut time, adding to the condition), [let Yahweh destroy me].

The effect of this is to swear that, as Yahweh lives, the servant will succeed by the help of Yahweh in securing a wife for Isaac from among Abraham's own people.

Selected Bibliography

I. HEBREW GRAMMAR AND SYNTAX

Alting, Jacob, *Fundamenta Punctationis Lingua Sancta*.
Frankfort-on-the-Main: Knochi & Eslingei, 1746.

Baer and Strack, *Die Dikduke ha-teamim des Ahron ben Moschek ben Ascher*.
Leipzig: 1879.

Blake, Frank Ringgold, *A Resurvey of Hebrew Tenses*.
Rome: Pontificium Institutum Biblicum, 1951.

Bush, George, *A Grammar of the Hebrew Language*.
New York: Leavitt, Lord & Company, 1835.

Carlson, E. Leslie, *Elementary Hebrew*.
Kansas City: Central Seminary Press, 1945.

Davidson, A. B., *An Introductory Grammar*.
Edinburgh: T. & T. Clark, 1900.
Davidson, A. B., *Hebrew Syntax*.
Edinburgh: T. & T. Clark, 1894.
Driver, G. R., *Problems of the Hebrew Verbal System*.
Edinburgh: T. & T. Clark, 1936.
Driver, S. R., *A Treatise on the Use of the Tenses in Hebrew*.
Oxford: The Clarendon Press, ed. 3, 1892.

Evans, D. Tyssil, *The Principles of Hebrew Grammar*.
London: Luzac and Company, 1912.
Ewald, Heinrich, *Syntax of the Hebrew Language*.
Edinburgh: T. & T. Clark (translated by James Kennedy), 1879.

Gray, George Buchanan, *The Forms of Hebrew Poetry*.
London: Hodder and Stoughton, 1915.
Green, Samuel C., *A Handbook of Old Testament Hebrew*.
London: The Religious Tract Society, 1921.
Green, William Henry, *A Grammar of the Hebrew Language*.
New York: John Wiley & Sons, revised ed., 1892.

Harper, William R., *Elements of Hebrew*.
New York: Charles Scribner's Sons, 1921.
Harper, William R., *Elements of Hebrew Syntax*.
New York: Charles Scribner's Sons, 1888.
Hurwitz, Hyman, *A Grammar of the Hebrew Language*.
London: John Taylor, ed. 2, 1835.

Kautzsch, E., editor and reviser, *Gesenius' Hebrew Grammar*.
Oxford: The Clarendon Press, ed. 28, 1910 (The first ed. appeared
at Halle, Germany in 1813. Twelve more editions were made by
W. Gesenius himself; ed. 14 to ed. 21 by E. Rödiger, ed. 22 to ed.
28 by E. Kautzsch; translated by A. E. Cowley).

Lee, S., *A Grammar of the Hebrew Language*.
London: James Duncan, 1827.

Mannheimer, S., *Hebrew Reader and Grammar*.
New York: Bloch Publishing Company, ed. 15, 1892.
Martin, Malachi, *The Scribal Character of the Dead Sea Scrolls*.
Louvain: Publications Universitaires, 1958.
Muller, August, *Outlines of Hebrew Syntax*.
Glasgow: James Maclehose and Sons (translated and edited by
James Robertson), 1882.

Naor, Menahem, *Iquare Hadiqduq Haivree*, (in Hebrew).
Haifa: Beth Sefer Hareali Maivree, 1937.

Ostborn, Gunnar, *Tora in the Old Testament* (a semantic study).
Lund: Hakan Ohlssons boktr., 1945.

Palache, Jehuda Leon, *Semantic Notes on the Hebrew Lexicon*.
Leiden: E. J. Brill (translated from the Dutch by R. J. Zwi Wer-
blowsky), 1959.

Qimhi, D., *Hebraicum Institutionem*, libri IV.
Paris: Robert Stephanus, 1549.

Reuchlin, Johann, *Rudimenta Linguae Hebraicae*.
Pforzheim: 1506.
Robinson, Theodore Henry, *The Poetry of the Old Testament*.
London: Duckworth, 1947.

Schroeder, N. G., *Institutiones ad Fundamenta Linguae Hebraicae*.
Stettiniana: In officina Librar, 1792.
Segal, M. H., *A Grammar of Mishnaic Hebrew*.
Oxford: The Clarendon Press, 1927.
Stuart, Moses, *A Grammar of the Hebrew Language*.
Andover: Flagg & Gould, 1831.

Weingreen, Jacob, *A Practical Grammar for Classical Hebrew*.
Oxford: The Clarendon Press, 1952.

Wickes, William, *A Treatise on the Accentuation of the Three So-Called Poetical Books of the Old Testament.*
Oxford: Clarendon Press, 1881.

Wood, C. T., and Lanchester, H. C. O., *A Hebrew Grammar.*
London: Kegan, Paul, Trench, Trubner & Co., Ltd., 1920.

Yates, Kyle M., *Essentials of Biblical Hebrew.*
New York: Harper and Brothers, ed. 4, 1938.

Yoder, Sanford Calvin, *Poetry of the Old Testament.*
Scottdale, Pa.: Herald Press, 1952.

Young, George Douglas, *Grammar of the Hebrew Language.*
Grand Rapids: Zondervan Publishing House, 1951.

II. HEBREW LEXICOGRAPHY AND CONCORDANCE

Brown, Driver and Briggs, *A Hebrew and English Lexicon of the Old Testament* (Based on the Lexicon of Wilhelm Gesenius as translated by Edward Robinson).
New York: Houghton Mifflin Company, 1906.

Buxtorf, John (the elder), *Thesaurus Grammaticus Linguae Sanctae Hebraicae.*
Basel: 1615.

Davidson, A. B., *A Concordance of the Hebrew and Chaldee Scriptures.*
London: Samuel Bagster and Sons (revised and corrected), 1876.

Furst, Julius, *A Hebrew & Chaldee Lexicon.*
Leipzig: Bernhardi Tauchnitz, ed. 3, (translated by S. Davidson), 1867.

Gesenius, Wilhelm, *Hebräisch-deutsches Handwörterbuch des Alten Testaments.*
Leipzig: 1810-1812.

Gesenius, Wilhelm, *Hebrew and Chaldee Lexicon to the Old Testament Scriptures.*
Grand Rapids: reprint, Wm. B. Eerdmans Publishing Co., translated and edited by Samuel Prideaux Tregelles, 1846-1857.

Gesenius, Wilhelm, *A Hebrew and English Lexicon of the Old Testament.*
Boston: Crocker and Brewster, (translated by Edward Robinson), 1836-1854.

Gesenius, Wilhelm, *Neues Hebräisches-deutsches Handwörterbuch.*
Leipzig: 1815-1828.

Gesenius, Wilhelm, *Thesaurus Philologicus Criticus Linguae Hebraeae et Chaldaeae Veteris Testamenti.*
Leipzig: 1829-1842.

Grossman and Segal, *Compendious Hebrew-English Dictionary.*
(Comprising a Complete Vocabulary of Biblical, Mishnaic, Medieval
and Modern Hebrew.)
Tel Aviv: Dvir Publishing Co., 1946.

Koehler, Ludwig, *Lexicon In Veteris Testamenti Libros.*
Vols. 1 & 2; Aramaic portions by Walter Baumgartner). Grand
Rapids: Wm. B. Eerdmans Publishing Co., 1953.

Mandelkern, Solomon, *Veteris Testamenti Concordantiae.*
Leipzig: Veit et Comp., 1896.

Parkhurst, John, *Hebrew and English Lexicon.*
London: William Baynes and Son, (a new ed., corrected, enlarged
and improved), 1923.

Roy, W. L., *A Complete Hebrew and English Critical and Pronouncing
Dictionary.*
New York: John F. Trow & Company, 1846.

Yehuda, Ben, *A Complete Dictionary of Ancient and Modern Classical
Hebrew.*
New York: Thomas Yoseloff, 1960.

Zorell, Franciscus, *Lexicon Hebraicum et Aramaicum Veteris Testamenti.*
Rome: Pontificum Institutum Biblicum, 1951.

III. ENGLISH GRAMMAR, SYNTAX
AND LEXICOGRAPHY

Curme, George O., *Syntax* (Vol. III of *A Grammar of the English
Language*).
New York: D. C. Heath and Company, 1931.

Opdycke, John B., *Harper's English Grammar.*
New York: Harper & Brothers, 1941.

Webster's New International Dictionary of the English Language.
(Harris, W. T., Editor-in-Chief; Allen, F. Sturges, General Editor.)
Springfield: G. & C. Merriam Co., 1932.

IV. MASORETIC TEXT

Baer, Seligman, *Biblia Hebraica.*
Leipzig: Bernhardi Tauchnitz, 1879.

Ginsberg, C. David, *Hebrew Bible.* (with text and critical apparatus
based upon the Bomberg Bible.)
London: Trinitarian Bible Society, 1894.

Ginsberg, C. David, *Introduction to the Hebrew Bible.*
London: Trinitarian Bible Society, 1897.

Kittel, Rud., *Biblia Hebraica.* (With masoretic text provided by P. Kahle.)
Stuttgart: Priv. Württ. Bibelanstlat, ed. 7, 1951.

Letteris, Maier Halevy, ...
London: British and Foreign Bible Society, 1890(?)-1937.

Simonis, Johannis, *Biblia Hebraica.*
Halle: ed. 4, 1828.

Van der Hooght, Everadi, *Biblia Hebraica.*
Leipzig: Bernhardi Tauchnitz, ed. 3, 1833.

V. TRANSLATIONS

American Standard Version.
Published in America in 1901 A.D.

An American Translation.
Made by J. M. Powis Smith and a group of scholars,
Chicago: University of Chicago Press, 1927.

Authorized Version.
Published in England in 1611 A.D.

Die Heilige Schrift.
Made by Emil Kautzsch and a group of scholars,
Elbefeld: R. Brochhaus, 1907.

Douay Version.
Published in England in 1609 A.D.
New York: P. K. Kenedy & Sons, 1941.

English Revised Version.
Published in England in 1885 A.D.

The Holy Bible from Ancient Eastern Manuscripts.
Containing Old & New Testaments.
Translated from the Peshitta, the Authorized Bible of the
Church of the East, by George M. Lamsa.
Philadelphia: A. J. Holman Company, 1957.

The Holy Bible in Modern English.
Written by Ferrar Fenton.
London: Adam & Charles Black, 1903.

*The Holy Scriptures According to the Masoretic Text,
A New Translation.*
Made by Jewish Scholars in America,
Philadelphia: The Jewish Publication Society of America, 1917.

The New English Bible.
  Oxford University Press;
  Cambridge University Press, 1963.

A New Translation.
  Made by James Moffatt,
  New York and London: Harper & Brothers, 1922.

New World Translation of the Hebrew Scriptures.
  Made by New World Translation Committee.
  Brooklyn: Watchtower Bible and Tract Society, 1953-1960.

Revised Standard Version.
  New York: Thomas Nelson & Sons, 1952.

The Septuagint.
  Made by Jews in Egypt about 275-150 B.C.
  Edited by Henry Barclay Swete.
  Cambridge: University Press, 1887-1934.

The Vulgate
  Made by Jerome in Palestine about 390-405 A.D.
  Contained in the Triglot Bible,
  London: Richard D. Dickinson, 1890.

Index of Biblical References

(The following references are given primarily with reference to the Hebrew Bible. If a reference in parentheses is given, it refers to English translations.)

VERSES	PAGE NUMBERS	VERSES	PAGE NUMBERS
GENESIS		2:19	61, 62
1:1	13, 18, 19, 30, 35, 36	3:1	22
1:1-3	109	3:6-16	109
1:2	13, 14, 15, 25, 35	3:10	25
1:3	82, 83, 111	3:11	76, 118
1:3-19	36	3:14	25, 88, 128
1:4	21	4:2	95, 101
1:6	83, 112	4:6	25
1:6-9, 15-19	61	4:7	25, 56
1:7	122, 123	4:8	133
1:9	82, 83	4:9	24
1:17, 18	96	4:10	16, 30, 72
1:26	36	4:14	30, 135
1:29	21	5:3	19, 61, 62
1:31	36	5:4	61, 62
1:1—2:3	61	5:5	16
2:2	30	5:6, 7, 9, 10, 12	
2:3	96	13, 15, 16, 18,	
2:4	94	19, 21, 22, 25,	
2:4-25	61	26, 28, 30	62
2:5	23, 61	6:1	95
2:6	17	6:2	18, 19
2:6-9, 15-19	61	6:4	26
2:6, 7	108, 109	6:9	37
2:7	20	6:9, 10	109
2:8	45, 122	6:13	17
2:10	48, 49	6:17	72, 73, 128
2:10-14	68	7:4	72, 73
2:15	23	7:20	20
2:17	89, 93, 101	8:7	93
2:18	94	8:8	24

157

Verses	Page Numbers	Verses	Page Numbers
9:3	120	27:4	130
9:13-16	115	28:42	22
9:24	21	28:13, 15	13, 15
9:25	22	28:20	14
9:26	26	28:20-22	139
10:14	123	29:30	22
11:18	95	30:13	39, 40
11:10-24	62	30:18	128
11:28	63	30:30	24
12:1	27, 62, 63, 64	30:34	84
12:9	93	31:13	63
12:13	130	32:11 (32:10)	45
13:10	17	32:27, 29	135
13:16	76, 141	32:31	20
14:10	22	33:8	24
14:21-23	38	33:13	135
15:12	98	33:18	19
15:13	123	35:13	122, 123
16:8	24	36:2	37
17:2	78, 79	37:5	21
17:16	39, 40	37:7	71
17:18	25	37:35	16, 20
17:20	50, 51, 52	38:11	131
18:1	19, 71	39:9	127
18:15	102	40:13	50, 51, 52
18:19	15	40:23	43
18:25	25	41:15	119
18:26	116	41:33	83
18:30	83	41:34	116
19:20	83	41:59	119
21:7	76	43:7	63
21:13	135	43:9	140
21:26	102	43:16	125
22:7	108	43:20, 23	25
22:12	128	44:22	135, 136
22:24	27	44:32	139
23:13	25	44:33	83
24:4	63	45:25	19
24:7	63, 116	46:2	20
24:15	120, 121	46:30	80
24:19	57	47:8	24
24:38	148, 149	47:29, 30	114
24:44	102	49:17, 18	84, 85
24:57	81	49:27	60
24:58	24	50:5	80
25:34	64, 65	50:50	112
26:13	93		

VERSES	PAGE NUMBERS
EXODUS	
1:7	43
1:16	135
2:6	26
2:10	110
2:13	24
3:1	70
3:3	78, 79
3:10	90, 129
3:11	77
3:14	67
3:16	116
3:18	80
3:19	44
4:7	89
4:13	125
4:16	57
4:18	129
5:16	15
5:23	131
6:3	20
6:6-8	113, 115
6:10	97
6:11	89
6:12	135
7:2	88
7:9	119
8:17 (8:21)	135
9:5	59
9:16	99
10:6	102
13:7	21
14:12	24
14:13	102
15:1	55, 59, 108
16:3	25
16:27	17
17:2	24
19:5	26
19:6	15
19:10-13	51, 52
19:13	102
20:3	89
20:8	91
20:8, 9	93
20:9	32, 88
20:10	32

VERSES	PAGE NUMBERS
20:12	32, 90
20:15	89
20:20	23
21:2-6	144
21:2-11	140
21:5	141
21:2-14	143, 145, 146
21:3, 8	147
21:18, 19	114
21:28	21, 93
23:9	128
29:9	20
31:14	16
33:8-11	16, 68, 117
33:16	98
34:6	26
34:18	102
LEVITICUS	
5:2-4	102
11:4	21
14:43, 44	131
17:11	27
26:45	101
NUMBERS	
12:1	16
14:2, 28	25
16:29	23
17:27 (17:12)	39, 40
20:12	128
20:21	94
22:30	131
22:33	75
23:10	75
23:19	129
24:9	16
24:17	41, 42, 59
35:23	23
36:4	139
DEUTERONOMY	
1:12	76
1:36	128
2:14	131
2:27	80

VERSES	PAGE NUMBERS	VERSES	PAGE NUMBERS
2:30	49	**I SAMUEL**	
2:34	21	1:3	96
4:1	72	1:7	56, 57
4:33	110	1:23	83
8:20	128	2:4	16
9:21	93	4:15	15
11:10	48, 49	5:9	20
12:23	15	8:19	102
15:3	81	9:3	21
17:14	78, 79	10:5	59
17:19, 20	23	10:19	118, 119
18:21	24	10:27	110
22:8	17	11:13	24
23:4, 5 (23:3, 4)	127	12:3	45
31:17	127	12:17	96
32:6, 21	23	14:10	46
32:27-29	137, 138	14:33	96
33:16	77	14:45	135, 148
		15:20	119
JOSHUA		15:32	20
3:1	131	16:3	125
3:14-16	98	16:7	57
3:14-17	132	17:14	22
6:8, 9	49	18:23	94
8:7	88	19:11	72
17:16	102	20:6	93
		20:21	59
JUDGES		20:22	31
2:1	58	21:15 (21:14)	25, 31, 59
5:18	97	23:20	25
7:13	71	24:21	59
8:19	74	25:43	101
13:7	24	26:16	22
13:23	137	26:21	128
14:10	56, 57	28:20	45
14:16	101	28:22	112
18:4	79	31:7	16
19:18	21		
20:44	22	**II SAMUEL**	
21:25	56, 57	1:4	17
		3:11	99
RUTH		3:16, 24	93
1:13	77	3:30	127
1:17	148	3:34	99
2:11	63	5:24	45
2:12	121	7:7	21
2:22	118	7:28	15, 17

VERSES	PAGE NUMBERS	VERSES	PAGE NUMBERS
11:11	148	5:20	135, 136
11:15	22	8:13	18, 19
12:23	73	10:5	124
13:36	21	20:1	97
14:5	110		
17:5	27	**I CHRONICLES**	
18:14	131	12:33 (12:32)	77
19:5	21		
20:21	73	**II CHRONICLES**	
23:15	24	24:14	95
24:22, 23	37		

I KINGS

		EZRA	
1:2	83	1:3	81, 82
1:11	38		
1:33-35	39	**NEHEMIAH**	
1:35	38, 39	2:2	93
2:1	98		
2:3	97	**ESTHER**	
3:1	98	7:2	82, 83
3:3	112	8:8	97
3:7	94		
3:16	58, 59 108	**JOB**	
4:14	22	1:1	124
7:8	45	1:3	22
8:1	58	1:15	27
8:1, 2	108	3:13	18
8:26	83	5:7	101
8:27-28	115	7:9	47
8:47	123	7:13-14	135
10:21	23	8:12	23
12:16	24	9:2	24
13:8	77	10:14	135
13:33	81, 82	11:18	15
15:23	22	18:21	125
17:25	22	22:12	128
18:17	27	24:19	102
18:29	98	34:5	44
18:32	19	34:29	102
20:8	81		
22:8	83	**PSALMS**	
22:30	92	1:1	47

II KINGS

		1:2	19, 55, 56
1:3	23	2:3	81
4:43	92	3:8	19
5:10	91, 92	4:7 (4:6)	17

VERSES	PAGE NUMBERS	VERSES	PAGE NUMBERS
4:9 (4:8)	80, 81	**SONG OF SONGS**	
9:21 (9:20)	119	1:8	22
14:7	84		
16:3	124	**ISAIAH**	
17:12	60	1:2	50, 115
20:4	77	1:3	46
24:3	77	1:3-4	45
24:10	24	1:4	31
25:2	80	1:7	72
27:2	27, 40	1:9	75, 137
31:7 (31:6)	44	1:11	57
31:15 (31:14)	44	1:15	15
32:3	131	1:16, 17	92
40:6	23	1:18	76, 81, 142
41:7 (41:6)	135	1:19, 20	139
44:27 (44:26)	90	1:20	20
46:3 (46:2)	98	2:2	51, 52
49:18	24	3:7	128
51:14 (51:12)	57, 90	3:15	24
55:15 (55:14)	56	3:16	128
56:3	20	4:3-4	45
67:7	42	4:4	139, 147
81:14-15 (81:13-14)	75, 138	5:2	110
103:5	16	5:4	24
110:5	42	5:5	116
119:113	47	5:6	99
119:136	127	5:9	23
119:137	15	5:11	132
126:2	17	5:13	42
139:14	20	5:19	77
139:19	25	5:20	25
		6:1	27
PROVERBS		6:8	21, 76
1:28, 29	128	6:9	26, 84, 85, 86
3:7	81	6:9, 10	84, 85, 86
8:17	57	6:13	97
19:8	97	7:11	91, 93, 94
22:23	20	7:13	94
25:16	135	7:14	27
		8:7	116
ECCLESIASTES		8:8	42, 116
1:16	115	9:1	42
3:4	95	9:5 (9:6)	41, 68
5:4	118	9:6	17
5:15	102	10:3, 4	31
7:14	130	10:28	42
12:6	84		

Verses	Page Numbers	Verses	Page Numbers
10:33	40	5:7	24
11:1-12:6	69	6:4	59
11:8	40	7:12	122
11:9	44	12:3	50
14:6	23	16:13	21
15:9	44	22:10	63
22:13	92	22:19	21
24:13	139	22:29	25
28:2	42	23:14	92
28:4	131	28:9	120
28:13	113, 116	30:21	76
28:25	139	31:36, 37	141
31:8	27	31:37	112
34:13	16	33:20, 21	141
37:16	27	42:2	17
37:28	94	46:16	63
38:10	80	52:7	31
40:7	47		
40:30	112	**LAMENTATIONS**	
41:7	21		
42:1	124	1:19	129
43:3, 4	127		
44:12	68	**EZEKIEL**	
45:14	82		
45:21	81, 82	17:21	22
46:4	101, 111, 129	23:15	63
47:1	15	40:1	131
49:3	121		
49:6	115	**HOSEA**	
50:4	21		
51:12	60	3:5	80
52:13-53:12	80	4:3	50
52:14, 15	102	4:6	42
53:1	75	7:4	98
53:1, 2	110, 128	11:4	82
53:5	18	11:9	80
53:10	44	13:14	78, 79, 80
53:12	42	14:5 (14:4)	57
55:1	23, 102		
55:7	96	**JOEL**	
62:1	60	1:6	23
65:1	126	1:15	25
		1:20	16
JEREMIAH		**AMOS**	
3:8	127	1:3	127
3:20	102	2:16	20

VERSES	PAGE NUMBERS	VERSES	PAGE NUMBERS
4:7	18	2:6	15
4:12	128	6:8	93
5:2	42		
5:3	20	**HAGGAI**	
5:15	112	2:11	20
JONAH		**ZACHARIAH**	
1:7	81	1:9	24
1:11	129	4:5	15
3:5	22	8:2	21
		14:4	20
MICAH		**MALACHI**	
1:2	84		
1:8, 9	85	2:2	139